Not One of the Family:
Foreign Domestic Workers in Canada
Edited by Abigail B. Bakan and Daiva Stasiulis

In *Not One of the Family*, workers-turned-activists and experts on foreign domestic workers document how the Canadian system has institution-alized unequal treatment of citizen and non-citizen workers. Since the 1940s rights of citizenship for immigrant domestic workers in Canada have declined, while the number of women recruited from Third World countries to work in Canadian homes has dramatically increased. The analysis in *Not One of the Family* is both theoretical and practical, fram-ing ideologies of privacy, maternalism, familialism, and rights, as well as examining government policy, labour organizing, and strategies to resist exploitation.

A key resource for all centres for women and immigrant workers, *Not One of the Family* is also essential reading for civil rights and immigra-tion lawyers, labour groups, and government policy makers.

ABIGAIL BAKAN is Associate Professor of Political Studies at Queen's University. She is the author of *Ideology and Class Conflict in Jamaica: The Politics of Rebellion*.

DAIVA STASIULIS is Professor of Sociology at Carleton University. She is the co-editor of *Unsettling Settler Societies: Articulations of Gender, Race, Ethnicity, and Class*.

Not One of the Family

Foreign Domestic Workers in Canada

Edited by
Abigail B. Bakan
and Daiva Stasiulis

UNIVERSITY OF TORONTO PRESS
Toronto Buffalo London

© University of Toronto Press Incorporated 1997
Toronto Buffalo London
Printed in Canada

ISBN 0-8020-0642-6 (cloth)
ISBN 0-8020-7595-9 (paper)

Printed on acid-free paper

Canadian Cataloguing in Publication Data

Main entry under title:
Not one of the family : foreign domestic workers in Canada

Includes bibliographical references and index.
ISBN 0-8020-0642-6 (bound) ISBN 0-8020-7595-9 (pbk.)

1. Women domestics – Canada.   2. Women alien labor –
Canada.   I. Bakan, Abigail B. (Abigail Bess), 1954–   .
II. Stasiulis, Daiva Kristina, 1954–   .

HD6072.2.C3N67 1997   331.4'8164046'0971   C97-930145-9

University of Toronto Press acknowledges the financial assistance to its
publishing program of the Canada Council and the Ontario Arts Council.

This book is dedicated to the memory of Flor Contemplacion.

Contents

Acknowledgments

The essays in this collection are brought together as part of a larger study directed by the editors on immigrant women and the role of North-South relations, race, gender, and class in constructing citizenship. This study has been made possible through the support of the Social Sciences and Humanities Research Council of Canada.

The support of a number of organizations and individuals has been invaluable in the completion of this volume.

We are grateful to Virgil Duff, executive editor at the University of Toronto Press, and to Bill Wood, our manuscript editor, for their invaluable assistance in preparing the manuscript for publication; to Wayne Daniels, for preparing the index; to Felicita Villasin, director of INTER-CEDE, for her support of this collection and our larger project; to Linda MacDougall, senior policy advisor at Citizenship and Immigration Canada, for making crucial data available to us when needed; and to the helpful comments provided by two anonymous readers. Maureen Rice provided impeccable research assistance in enabling us to complete the manuscript.

While in the Philippines, Hong Kong, and Singapore, conducting research in the spring of 1995, we were welcomed into the homes and offices of numerous activists fighting for the rights of Filipino women migrants. Particular thanks are owed to Gabriela, Migrante, Batis, BAYAN, Kanlungan, and the family of the late Flor Contemplacion, to the memory of whom this book is dedicated. We are particularly indebted to Pura Velasco, who blazed a path for us through her home country of the Philippines as our guide, interpreter, and organizer. She helped us gain a glimpse into the world that so many domestic workers here in Canada have left behind in hopes of building a better future. The support of the Philippines Solidarity Group and the Coalition for the Defense of Migrant Workers' Rights in Canada, in which Pura is an active member, has also greatly facilitated the research for this book.

We are immensely grateful to Paul Kellogg and Radha Jhappan, whose support of our work has been substantial, constant, and unconditional.

Any errors are ours alone.

Contributors

SEDEF ARAT-KOC is Associate Professor, Women's Studies and Department of Sociology, Trent University.

ABIGAIL B. BAKAN is Associate Professor, Political Studies, Queen's University.

PATRICIA M. DAENZER is Associate Professor and Director, Women's Studies, McMaster University.

MIRIAM ELVIR is a member of L'Association pour la Défense des Droits du Personnel Domestique [The Association for the Defence of the Rights of Domestic Workers].

JUDY FUDGE is Associate Professor, Osgoode Hall Law School, York University.

DAIVA STASIULIS is Professor, Department of Sociology and Anthropology, Carleton University.

PURA M. VELASCO is a founding member of the Coalition for the Defence of Migrant Workers' Rights.

Not One of the Family

Introduction

ABIGAIL B. BAKAN and DAIVA STASIULIS

On 17 March 1995, Flor Contemplacion, a forty-two-year-old Filipino mother of four who had been working as a nanny in Singapore, was executed. Ms Contemplacion had been convicted for the double murder in 1991 of Delia Maga, another Filipino nanny, and the four-year-old son of Maga's Singaporean employer. Based on independent interviews with the condemned woman, and evidence from the exhumed body of Ms Maga, many Filipinos believed that Ms Contemplacion was innocent of any wrongdoing. According to an official Philippine government commission report, this was an 'execution that could have been prevented' had this evidence been allowed to come forward in Flor Contemplacion's defence (Gancayco 1995, Part Four, 12).

Ms Contemplacion, who had been visiting her friend Ms Maga, is widely believed to have been framed and tortured into confessing in order to direct suspicion away from the real murderer. Available evidence points to Ms Maga's employer, a Singaporean citizen, as the actual prime suspect.[1] The questionable conviction of Ms Contemplacion, her death sentence, and the rejection by the Singaporean government of a stay of execution requested by Philippine President Fidel Ramos, enraged millions of Filipinos, who denounced the ruthless Singaporean judicial system (Gancayco 1995; Safire 1995; Tesher 1995).

For many Filipinos, Flor Contemplacion became a martyr. The level of political protest that this case generated has been compared to the ferment preceding the fall of the Marcos dictatorship. Indeed, although the execution took place on the order of a Singapore court, and 'protest actions against the Singaporean government ensued,' including the torching of thousands of Singaporean flags, even according to the government-appointed commissioners, 'a louder clamour was made against some Filipino government officials mandated by law to give overseas Filipinos adequate protection while abroad' (Gancayco 1995, Introduction, 1; Sherwell 1995, A9). In the face of outrage expressed by political groups ranging from the extreme left to the Christian right, President Ramos hailed Ms Contemplacion a national heroine. His wife, Amelita, was present at the Manila airport to join supporters awaiting the return of Contemplacion's body. The incident prompted a diplomatic crisis between the two Southeast Asian neighbours as both countries withdrew their ambassadors.

While symbolically defiant, the response from the Ramos government also revealed restraint. Indeed, the groundswell of opposition to the conviction of Flor Contemplacion was so great that the Philippine government was compelled to publicly express concern. Its caution in doing so, however, reflected the Ramos administration's fear of jeopardizing the considerable investments by its wealthier Asian neighbours in the chronically indebted and underdeveloped Philippine economy, and its dependence for foreign exchange and survival on the contract labour export of one-tenth of its population. Labour export was originally viewed as a temporary answer to chronic unemployment and severe balance of payments problems in the Philippines. However, the export of workers, and in particular international trafficking in female domestics, nannies, entertainers, prostitutes, and mail-order brides, has now become an integral aspect of the Philippines political economy. All administrations since Marcos have been determined not to upset this lucrative program of labour export (Gibson and Graham 1986; Angeles 1993, 1).[2]

At first glance, the execution of a Filipino nanny in Singapore might appear totally removed from the condition of foreign nannies and other migrant household workers living in Canada. The postcolonial Singaporean regime of Lee Kuan Yew combines capitalist prosperity in an economy dominated by foreign multinationals with a sexist and racialist (pro-Chinese majority) authoritarian rule (Heng and Devan 1992).[3] Lee Kuan Yew has maintained power and stifled opposition by aggrandizing the state and party with social welfare measures. There has also been ample use of anti-terrorism laws left over from the British, who originally used them to quell communist insurgency in Malaysia in the 1950s. In the context of the Pacific Rim, where booming economies have created high demand for foreign 'domestic helpers,' this city-state is widely regarded to impose the most restrictive and repressive conditions on migrant maids in Asia (Medel-Anonueva, Abad-Sarmiento and Oliveros-Vistro 1989, 166).

Thus, domestic helpers in Singapore are obliged to sign a Statement of Undertaking that prohibits them from marrying or cohabiting with any Singaporean citizen or permanent resident. In addition, foreign domestic workers are forbidden from becoming pregnant, and are required to submit to a pregnancy test every six months. If found pregnant, a worker is immediately deported to her country of origin.[4] Their passports are withheld by employers and twenty per cent of their earnings are held back by their employers in order to cover the costs of their return passage. The employment contract signed with employers provides for only one day off a month, after three months of probation. Migrant domestics cannot leave the country before the expiry of the two-year contract without release papers from the employer, and they are limited to four years' stay in Singapore.

There are no labour laws protecting domestic workers in Singapore. Domestic workers, including the five to ten runaways per week sheltered in a centre supported by the Philippine embassy, report a high incidence of gross employer abuses. These include severe cases of verbal, psychological, physical, and sexual harassment and abuse, including rape; imprisonment in the employer's home; substandard food and accommodation; labour abuse, including non-payment, delay, or underpayment of wages; excessive work hours and no overtime pay; and other contract violations. Singaporean state authorities are generally dismissive of the domestics' allegations of employer abuse, and consistently side with employers' versions of events. In 1988, the numerous complaints of maltreatment filed by Filipino domestics against their Singaporean employers resulted in a three-month ban on Filipino contract workers in Singapore, an action which the Philippine government has since periodically considered reimposing ('Hundreds' 1990).

Abuse and extreme exploitation of 'domestic helpers' (the more common term for domestic or household workers in Asia and the Middle East) is not confined to any one country, however. In 1995 alone, Migrante, an international alliance of Filipino migrant workers, reported a total of 40,971 cases of physical, sexual, and labour abuse involving Filipino migrant workers occurring in various countries around the globe, particularly in Asia and the Middle East. Many of these were domestic helpers (Migrante 1996, 1).[5]

In contrast to this documented pattern of pervasive migrant domestic abuse, Canada is internationally known to have more liberal policies and tolerable conditions for foreign domestic workers. A preference for working in Canadian households is clearly expressed by many Filipino domestics.[6] Those who have had prior experience working under abysmal conditions as domestics in Hong Kong, Singapore, or the Middle East widely view Canada to be among the most favourable emigration sites (see Pura Velasco, this volume).[7] This more liberal regime for foreign domestics ostensibly flows from Canada's status as a humane, multicultural, liberal democracy. Canada presents itself as an internationally recognized upholder of human and minority rights. Although exempt from many of the protections available to other workers, foreign domestics in Canada are covered by some employment standards regulated by the provinces. A major difference between the state treatment of foreign domestics in Canada as compared with most other countries is that after two years of working as household workers, foreign domestics are able to have an open working visa, permitting them to work in any occupation, and to qualify to apply for landed immigrant status.

Documented cases of chattel-like treatment, such as imprisonment in the employer's home, are much more rare in Canada than in countries in East Asia and the Gulf Region, where human-rights organizations have consistently found an alarmingly high incidence of virtual or actual enslavement of Asian maids (Gancayco 1995; Angeles 1993: Middle East Watch Women's Rights Project 1992).[8] Nonetheless, challenging cases of employer abuse of various types (physical, verbal, sexual) of live-in domestics forms a regular part of the workload of domestic advocacy groups in Canadian cities. In London, Ontario, the Urban Alliance, a coalition of race and ethnic organizations, reported in 1992 that during the previous six years, it had 'helped 21 domestic workers leave abusive situations, some involving sexual assault' ('Domestic Worker' 1992).

In Toronto, a study by INTERCEDE found that it was not uncommon for domestic workers to be fired without notice. In fact, as Judy Fudge (this volume) notes, several workers 'recounted experiences of being thrown out on the street, some at night and in the middle of winter.' The situation whereby employers have locked out their domestic workers, and denied them access both to their domicile and belongings, was sufficiently commonplace for members of the Vancouver-based West Coast Domestic Workers' Association to form a 'Domestic Emergency Response Team' (DERT), which would go on rescue missions of domestics who had experienced this form of abuse.

While some foreign household workers say 'Canada is heaven' compared with conditions for domestic helpers in countries like Singapore,[9] the fact that the outcry over Flor Contemplacion's execution was also heard among Filipino domestics in Canada reflected more than grief over the injustice meted out 'to one of their own' (Tesher 1995). The candlelit vigil in Metro Toronto attended by over one hundred Filipinos, many of them nannies, expressed an empathy for Contemplacion's fate and support for challenges to the injustices globally experienced by migrant domestic workers, whether employed in Singapore, Hong Kong, Abu Dhabi, Rome, Toronto, or Montreal.

In this book, we demonstrate that the similarities in the social and political status of migrant household workers in Canada, a liberal democratic society, with the status of such workers in non-democratic, less democratic, or illiberal societies, overrides the differences. Canada shares with more authoritarian regimes a glaring willingness and indeed determination to exploit female domestic migrant workers from developing countries whose limited wage-earning options have made them particularly vulnerable to political and legal control. Unlike other immigrant workers for whom there is a similarly high occupational demand,[10] foreign domestics are granted only temporary 'visitor' rather than landed immigrant status upon arrival. In addition, they are legally obliged to live in the households of their employers, a condition which undermines their civil liberties and heightens their vulnerability to every form of abuse. In every province where they work, private household workers have access only to partial and unregulated employment standards in comparison with those protecting the majority of workers. This makes Canadian domestic workers vulnerable to a similar range of abusive conditions experienced by domestic helpers in Singapore or Kuwait, including contract violations, inadequate pay and benefits, sexual harassment, and racism.

This collection of essays documents the historical, political, ideological, legal, and experiential dimensions of Canada's treatment of foreign domestics. We demonstrate that these various dimensions of oppression differ only in degree rather than in kind from the intolerable treatment received by migrant household workers the world over.

Foreign domestic workers are by no means the only group of workers or migrants in Canada to experience injustice and discrimination by virtue of their subordinate location within intersections of racial, gender, class, and neocolonial relations. Homeworkers, who tend to be non-English-speaking immigrant women (Borowy, Gordon, and Lebans 1993), contract agricultural seasonal workers from Jamaica and Mexico (Satzewich 1991), many Third World refugees, and sponsored immigrants[11] are also deprived of many of the benefits available to non-immigrant workers and citizens. International banking and corporate interests, in both their home and receiving states, as well as employers, treat domestic workers as 'peripheral.' Their lives are filled with uncertainties regarding even the most basic residential, financial, or familial considerations. The legal and political framework for migrant domestics can thus be viewed as illustrative of the trend toward 'global apartheid' (Richmond 1994). Immigration and refugee policies of prosperous countries are increasingly designed to attempt to protect their dominant status internationally, and the hegemony of dominant ethnic groups domestically. This arises in the face of overwhelming political, economic, and demographic pressures from underdeveloped societies in Asia, Africa, and Latin America to accept growing numbers of migrants. In the instance of foreign domestics, the majority of whom are migrant Third World women of colour, a number of economic, social, and political interests – the International Monetary Fund, the governments of sending countries of domestic workers, the Canadian federal and provincial states, private recruitment and placement agencies, and employers – are complicit in policing their access to the fruits of First World citizenship (Enloe 1989; Bakan and Stasiulis 1995, this volume).

This book explores the historical development and contemporary makeup of Canadian policies bringing in and regulating migrant domestics. The chapters by Sedef Arat-Koc and Patricia Daenzer reveal how ever greater restrictions were placed on foreign domestics' rights and freedoms as the sources for migrants shifted from Europe to the Third World, from white women to women of colour. Far from representing 'heaven,' the Live-in Caregiver Program (LCP), the Canadian federal program for foreign domestics since 1992, and its predecessor, the Foreign Domestic Movement (FDM), are viewed by many overseas, particularly Third World, household workers as a 'kind of necessary purgatory to obtain permanent residence' (Bals 1990, 158). A central theme of this book is an exploration of the ways in which the Canadian regulatory regime for migrant domestics violates international labour and human rights standards by institutionalizing unequal treatment between citizens and non-citizen/migrant workers in wages, working and living conditions, and access to rights.

A second theme is the active role taken by foreign domestics in efforts to subvert and change the policies and structures that exploit migrant household workers. The accounts of Miriam Elvir and Pura Velasco of their own experiences as domestic workers document how live-in domestics struggle daily to resist the control, surveillance, demeaning behaviour, and labour abuse by employers. They do so by refusing to comply with demands by employers for deferential behaviour, excessive hours of work, and unremunerated services. Wherever possible, they leave bad or abusive employers for those they believe will provide better wages and working conditions, as well as a modicum of respect. Moreover, domestic workers in Canada have effectively organized to resist the abuses of both employers and the state, as these narratives document.

Class, gendered, and racial struggles found in most public workplaces are expressed in forms of resistance that are 'structured, rule-governed and collective' (Romero 1992, 30–1). The class and racial antagonisms between a domestic worker and her employer, however, are often played out on an interpersonal level. The threats invoked by many employers of dismissal and deportation hinder, rather than prevent, individual acts of resistance by live-in household workers. Such threats are institutionalized in Canadian immigration policy. They often work to maintain the compliance of foreign domestics to unreasonable employer demands and inhumane treatment. This is precisely because these workers hold the status of temporary visitors on work visas. Their legal temporary residence in the country, as well as their chances of becoming a landed immigrant and gaining permanant legal status, are entirely contingent upon continued service as live-in household workers (Macklin 1992; 1994).

Efforts to change the immigrant status of foreign domestic workers to allow them to come in as landed immigrants rather than temporary workers have also been at the centre of collective struggles led by domestic advocacy organizations. The Toronto-based INTERCEDE (originally an acronym for International Coalition to End Domestics' Exploitation), the Montreal-based Association pour La Défense des Droits du Personnel Domestique, and the Vancouver-based West Coast Domestic Workers' Association are some of the largest of these organizations. As the chapter in this volume by Judy Fudge documents, collective struggles that involve domestic advocacy groups working in alliance with other immigrant and feminist groups, progressive lawyers, and trade unionists have also sought coverage by provincial employment standards of domestic workers on a par with those of other workers. Effective unionization and collective bargaining have long been elusive goals for domestics because of the 'special' features of paid domestic work, especially as it is performed by live-in workers on temporary visas (Epstein 1983).

It is useful to explore further the peculiar features of private domestic service that set it apart from the vast majority of jobs performed by wage workers in modern industrialized economies. In the remainder of this introduction, we will explore these features, focusing on the relations between material conditions, dominant discourses, and state regulation.

Familial Ideology, Maternalism, and Unfree Labour

The content of domestic workers' jobs and experiences in Canada and globally varies considerably. Nonetheless, the descriptions of the working conditions and key features of the employer-employee relations show remarkable similarity across time and space. Paid domestic labour 'is not seen as "real" work, nor are the people who do it seen as "real" workers' (Epstein 1983, 223). The low regard held of paid domestic work is an extension of the invisibility and low status of unpaid household work performed by women.

In addition to the low status, long hours, isolation, and poor pay and benefits associated with domestic service, many authors have commented on the affective, quasi-familial, and asymmetrical relations that develop between employers and (especially live-in) domestic employees (Anderson 1991; Bals 1990; Childress 1986; Colen 1989; Enloe 1989; Macklin 1992; Rollins 1985; Romero 1992). Private household work distinguishes itself from other service sector work,[12] and waged work in capitalist economies more generally. The personalized relations and non-work related bonds of attachment that commonly, and indeed often inevitably, exist between employers and employees are a feature of paid domestic service. The intimacy that prevails in this relationship is encapsulated in the oft-heard phrase uttered by employers that 'their' domestic worker or nanny is treated as 'one of the family,' or 'just like a daughter' (Anderson 1991; Childress 1986; Enloe 1989; Radcliffe 1990, 385; Romero 1992, 124). The imposition of compulsory live-in status for foreign domestics entering through the Live-in Caregiver Program means that migrant household workers in Canada are susceptible to the redefinition of work relations as familial-like obligations.

The characterization of relations with their employers as familial or quasi-familial is one adopted by some live-in domestic workers.[13] Those engaged in child care are particularly apt to develop an attachment to the employers' children, who may in turn come to view them as a 'second mother' (Bals 1990, 113). Whether performed for love or money, child care involves emotional labour associated with nurturing, care, guidance, and training (Colen 1989, 180). There are, however, perils attached to the development of maternal feelings among live-in child-care workers for their employers' children. As Colen cautions, 'Emotional care-giving to children who are not one's own ... can lead to emotional exploitation and vulnerability' (1989, 184). Employers are often willing to exploit the maternal and familial feelings of their employees in order to extract more hours of work from them, or to keep them in jobs which they might otherwise be inclined to leave earlier (Colen 1989, 184; Silvera 1983).

Many household workers have firmly rejected the notion that they are part of their employer's family on the grounds that such kinship-like idioms mask their actual subordinate status and position in their employer's household.[14] As super-exploited migrant workers, under the constant surveillance of their employers, foreign domestics lack many of the options and protections available to other workers, including those working within service industries. As members of the household, but most emphatically not members of the family, private domestic workers lack the benefits normally accorded to adult family members. Yet domestic workers are frequently expected to take on many stressful 'family' responsibilities and burdens of a family that is not their own. As Mary Romero puts it, 'Their objections to the analogy [of family member] are related to the employer's distortion of the real basis of their relationship which results in the extraction of unpaid physical and emotional labor' (1992, 124).

A second reason for rejecting the family member analogy is that it obscures the fact that domestic workers have families of their own. The families of these workers are spatially divided, sometimes over thousands of miles. They are made to sustain various pressures as a result of restrictive Canadian immigration policies that do not allow family members to accompany foreign domestics to Canada. The denial of family life to migrant domestic workers is an intrinsic aspect of the state policies constraining the rights of these workers.

The essays in this book reveal the reality behind the myth of the live-in foreign domestic worker as 'one of the family.' Such a characterization grossly distorts the objective economic, political, legal, and social conditions, and the class-based relations between employers and foreign domestics, that exist on a global scale. In this collection, our focus is the Canadian case in particular. Familial ideology has been demonstrated to be significant in contributing to women's social, economic, and sexual subordination, particularly among women whose experiences of 'family' do not conform to the idealized image. The dominant model of families, maintained and reinforced by law and state policies, is nuclear, heterosexual, with a male breadwinner, dependent female and children; it tends also to be white and middle class (Gavigan 1992; German 1994; Cossman 1992). Familial ideology is likely to have different and more acutely oppressive consequences for women whose roles are cast solely as providing aid in reproducing other (ideally white, middle class) families rather than as direct (re)producers of families.

The tenacity of assumptions about the relationship of migrant domestics to employer families in shaping labour relations for domestics both in Canada and globally makes it necessary to ask how and why it is that domestic workers become caught in this oppressive web of familial ideology. An answer to this question involves conceptually distinguishing families from households. In the case of foreign domestic workers, familial ideology ascribes ambiguous membership within employing families to workers who are members of employer's households, but not members of their families.

Foreign household workers normally provide service for several adult and child members of an employing family. Yet given that it is women who continue to bear primary responsibility for household labour, including child care, it is normally women who directly supervise the paid household worker. The asymmetrical relationship between women, which is further heightened by their divergent positions in hierarchies of class and race/ethnicity, has made paid domestic service a focus of particular interest to scholars of women's oppression (Arat-Koc 1989; Enloe 1989, 179; Macklin 1994, 30–7; Bakan and Stasiulis 1995; Romero 1992, 15). When women enter the paid labour force, they do not generally relinquish their responsibilities for child care and housework, thus leading to the 'double day.' The impression left by much of the literature on domestic service is that women, including feminists, who try to escape aspects of sexism (such as the double day) by paying others to perform household work are in denial of their contributory roles in the exploitation of poor women of colour. Isis Duarte (1989, 199) has suggested that the very presence of a paid domestic worker discourages the redistribution of household responsibilities and tasks within the family.[15] By establishing 'a new chain of hierarchical subordination ... in the family: husband/wife/domestic worker,' paid domestic service thus reaffirms a gendered division of labour, as well as introducing global/

racial/ethnic/class hierarchies into the heart of the family. As Cynthia Enloe succinctly asks, 'Isn't "feminist domestic employer" a contradiction' (1989, 179)?

As first suggested by David Katzman (1978b), and elaborated by Judith Rollins (1985, 178), what lies at the core of the contemporary relationship between female domestic employees and female employers is 'maternalism.' This differs from the paternalistic relationships between masters and servants first developed in feudal economies in Europe, and later transmitted to Third World countries and settler societies such as Canada under colonialism (Romero 1992, 49). As defined by Romero, 'Paternalism is at root a familial relation, and masters expected servants to demonstrate filial loyalty and obedience in return for protection and guidance' (1992, 49).

Rollins argues that maternalism is a more appropriate term than paternalism because the majority of contemporary employers of domestics in Western, and indeed non-Western, countries are women, and because women have altered the dynamic of paternalism in distinctly gendered ways (Romero 1992, 49). In the context of unequal power relations between employer and employee, the apparently caring, nurturing, and empathetic values of women employers become double-edged. They offer a potential for mutual emotional benefits, but also for curtailing the rights and freedoms of adult employees. As Rollins explains,

> The maternalism dynamic is based on the assumption of a superordinate-subordinate relationship. While maternalism may protect and nurture, it also degrades and insults. The 'caring' that is expressed in maternalism might range from an adult-to-child to a human-to-pet kind of caring but, by definition, ... it is not human-to-equal-human caring. The female employer, with her motherliness and protectiveness and generosity, is expressing in a distinctly feminine way her lack of respect for the domestic as an autonomous, adult employee. (1985, 186)

A dialectic of 'intimacy and depersonalization' that inscribes the maternalism dynamic in relations between workers and their employers manifests itself in patterned asymmetrical behaviours involving forms of address, space, physical appearance, and gift-giving (Colen 1989, 180; see also Silvera 1983; Rollins 1985; Romero 1992). Asymmetrical naming practices, whereby workers are called by their first names, or referred to as 'girls' regardless of their age, yet are expected to address their female employers as Mrs, Miss, or Ms, is a common form of linguistic deference in domestic service (Rollins 1985, 158–63).[16] Studies of household workers in Latin America reveal the pervasive use by employers of diminutive terms such as *chica, hija,* and *muchacha,* all variants on the terms 'girl' or 'daughter,' to address domestic workers, regardless of the age of these employees (Radcliffe 1990, 385; Castro 1989, 121).

While most modern middle-class North American homes are not built with 'spatial deference' (such as separate servant's entrances and rooms) in mind, live-in domestics generally are expected to render themselves invisible through their spatial practices (Romero 1992, 117). Household workers are often confined to particular parts of the house – such as the kitchen – when not explicitly working. They are expected to respect the privacy of employers, while themselves being denied privacy (Romero 1992, 117). This spatial segregation might extend to eating arrangments so that household workers would be expected to eat separately, and often only after their employers had eaten (Romero 1992, 118–19; Colen 1989, 181). The expectation that domestic workers render themselves invisible is, according to Katzman (1978b), rooted in the racial etiquette of the American South established under slavery. In such conditions, the 'ideal servant ... would be invisible and silent, responsive to demands but deaf to gossip, household chatter, and conflicts, attentive to the needs of mistress and master but blind to their faults, sensitive to the moods and whims of those around them but undemanding of family warmth, love, or security' (quoted in Romero 1992, 78).

The wearing of uniforms is another clear instance of a practice that maintains social distance between members of the employing household and private household workers, and signifies the inferior status of the employee. Romero remarks that 'in the past, employers sometimes insisted that domestics wear attire to match the table cloth or styles ranging from bright plaids and red dotted Swiss formal attire to a 1942 version of a beloved Southern Mammy's costume' (1992, 113). Miriam Elvir (this volume) recounts how she refused to acquiesce to the demand by her wealthy employers to wear a uniform at all times while in the house, including her off-work hours, regarding such a demand as an infringement on her autonomy and privacy.

The meeting of employer preferences in appearance of domestics is a highly racialized process. Racial stereotyping is the stock and trade of domestic placement agencies. One Toronto-based agency owner explained the rejection by one (presumably white) client of a black 'girl' sent by the agency on the basis of his dislike of the worker's hairdo, 'all in little braids' (Bakan and Stasiulis 1995, 311). The capacity of employers to select and reject domestics on the basis of their physical appearance, or to request changes in their employee's appearance even when not performing paid labour, illustrates the enormous control exercised by employers over workers in areas normally regarded to be private in capitalist wage relations.

The ubiquitous employer convention of giving 'gifts' to employees is perhaps the clearest instance of the maternalism dynamic in the employer-domestic employee relationship (Rollins 1985, 189). The giving of gifts bestows psychological benefits on the employer, providing her with the sense that she is benevolent, caring and kind to her employee. The nature of the gifts – cast-off clothing, discarded appliances and furniture, decorative baubles, even left-over food – establishes the gift-giving practice as a symbolically loaded one. Rather than expressing unbridled employer generosity, it usually is designed to establish the domestic employee's inferiority. This is especially the case given that such gifts are often provided in lieu of wage raises and benefits. Among other messages, this practice conveys 'the employer's perception of the servant as needy, unable to provide adequately for herself and willing to accept others' devalued goods' (Rollins 1985, 193). Unlike other forms of gift-giving, which involve reciprocity between parties exchanging gifts, gift-giving in domestic service occurs only in one direction. One-way gift-giving thus places the domestic under obligation to the employer to perform additional physical and emotional labour (Rollins 1985, 192; Romero 1992, 122).

In sum, maternalism, as expressed in various forms of spatial and linguistic deference, status-differentiating uniforms, and conventions of gift-giving, permits employers to exercise a degree of control over the lives, personhood, and autonomy of household workers considered unthinkable in most public employment situations. Indeed, such control often exceeds the degree of supervision of young middle-class women living in the same household (Radcliffe 1990). Sedef Arat-Koc (this volume) describes the close monitoring of English and Scottish domestics recruited during the early twentieth century by British-Canadian middle- and upper-class female reformers. The latter sought to protect the private virtues of young women brought over to do double duty as domestics and as future wives of British settler men (see also Barber 1986b).

Control over household workers' sexuality continues to be an intrinsic element of the regulation by employers of live-in domestics' personal lives. When they are not the victims of sexual abuse by males in the employing household (Silvera 1983), live-in workers are frequently treated as asexual beings by their employers, forbidden to receive guests in their rooms. They are often curtailed in their opportunity to leave the employer's home and pursue intimate relations or even friendships (Castro 1989, 120). The living space for the majority of live-in domestics in Canadian middle-class homes is not, in any case, designed to provide the privacy and separation from the employer's family required to engage in sexual and familial relations (West Coast Domestic Workers' Association 1989b, 4; Arat-Koc and Villasin 1990).

The regulation of migrant domestics' sexuality is also an important means through which foreign domestics are prevented from establishing their own families in their 'host' country. The extreme case of such regulation is the compulsory pregnancy test referred to earlier, to which migrant domestic workers in Singapore must submit every six months – one facet of the eugenics policies introduced by Lee Kuan Yew (Heng and Devan 1991, 349).[17] It should be recalled, however, that negative eugenics, the discouragement of settlement and reproduction of members of 'undesirable races,' has also historically been an integral feature of Canadian immigration policy. Thus, the Caribbean Domestic Scheme of the mid-1950s to 1960s specified that only single women with no dependants were permitted to come to Canada as landed immigrants, on condition that they remain in live-in domestic service for at least one year (Calliste 1989, 145). Such blatant eugenics features have since formally been removed from Canadian immigration domestic programs, largely because of the effective protests by domestics and their advocates in cases such as the 'Seven Jamaican Mothers' (see Judy Fudge this volume). Nonetheless, the preference for foreign domestics who are unencumbered by family responsibilities continues to be conveyed by Canadian immigration authorities overseas. As a result, to this day, applicants are under pressure to misrepresent their marital status and to hide the presence of children (Arat-Koc 1992, 242; West Coast Domestic Workers' Association 1989b, 3).[18]

Employment in live-in domestic service involves a break not only with the migrant woman's family of birth (natal family), but also with a household created by the woman with her partner and/or children (Radcliffe 1990, 386). This separation is all the more stark as it may exist over thousands of miles and several years, with no guarantee that the family will be reunited through successful sponsorship. The majority of surveys of foreign domestics reveal that homesickness, feelings of loneliness, guilt, and anxiety about children and other family members overseas are among the most common emotional problems experienced by migrant household workers (Colen 1989, 186; Alcid et al. n.d.).

The impact of migration on spouses and children who remain in the home country in the care of one parent or extended family has received little systematic research attention (Cox 1990). Some studies of returnee contract workers in the Philippines and Indonesia indicate that migrant workers and their families feel that the financial benefits offset the family problems resulting from the experience (Alcid et al. n.d.; Cox 1990, 136). Nonetheless, impressionistic evidence suggests that prolonged absences of migrant women may cause great emotional stress for spouses, left behind to shoulder the burden of single parenting and problems related to neglect of children (Torres-Calud n.d., 71; Cox 1990, 136).

The contradiction of long and painful separation from their own family members in order to care for another's is heightened by the fact that most domestic workers migrate in order to support their families financially and secure a better future for their children (Lycklama 1989, 43). Indeed, women from the West Indies, which in the 1970s constituted the largest Third World source region for foreign domestics in Canada, were often solely responsible for the financial welfare of their children (Silvera 1983, 19). The gendered, familial ideologies of the cultures of some sending societies may also contribute to the separation of female migrants from their families. There is an identified notion of the 'good daughter' in Philippine culture, for example, defined by her ability to bring income to her family (Angeles 1993, 19; Aguilar 1988).

Yet it would be wrong to assume that such separations are a matter of choice. The denial of entry to the children and partners of foreign domestics, and the forced separation of families through Canadian immigration programs such as the LCP, expose dramatically the racism of official state discourses that speak of the 'sanctity of families.' The 'family' that is to be protected from unnecessary state intervention is the middle-class white Canadian family. The same state shows no hesitation in disrupting the family lives of usually poor, rural women from developing countries.

The severe restrictions on the personal freedoms of live-in domestic workers delineated above has prompted a number of writers to label their status as 'feudal-like' or akin to slavery or indentured labour (Aitken 1987; Arat-Koc 1989). Such characterizations underline the construction of migrant household workers as one form, perhaps the most common for women in the world economic system, of unfree wage labour (Miles 1987). Unlike free labour, where labour power is exploited primarily through economic compulsion, unfree labour is heavily regulated through politico-legal state measures (Miles 1987, 181–6). The state, most prominently within the receiving society, is a leading force in the recruitment of unfree domestic migrants, and of enforcing relations of unfreedom. This is done chiefly through the denial of access of these workers to citizenship rights within the receiving nation-state. It remains to examine the links between the state's role in constituting migrant household workers as unfree labour, and state discourses on familial relations.

Familial Ideology and Paternalism in State Discourses

While maternalism pervades the treatment of live-in household workers by female employers, the regulation by state legislation and authorities of foreign domestics is often paternalistic. What both maternalism and (state or interpersonal) paternalism share in common is the treatment of the domestic worker as childlike and dependent. Thus, the Ministry of Interior's Director of Police Investigations in Kuwait dismissed the concerns raised by the common practice among employers of withholding the passports of their migrant Asian domestic employees, arguing, 'If an employer keeps the passport, it is only so the employee won't lose it, not to keep them in custody. It is just as we treat our children at home – it's the same thing with the maids.'[19]

The equation of nation-state pride with gendered stereotypes of male superiority surfaced in the response to a ban on the migration of Filipino maids to Saudi Arabia. This temporary ban was placed by then President Marcos of the Philippines following a finding of widespread abuse of Asian maids in that country. The Saudi Arabian ambassador reportedly protested 'that this would be an affront to Saudi manhood,' a classic example of the ideological construction of state paternalism (Lycklama 1989, 33–4).

In Canada, the ideology of the male-dominated, heterosexual nuclear family has informed a 'sweeping range of legislative initiatives as apparently disparate as child protection and minimum wages' (Gavigan 1992; see also Ursel 1992; Chunn 1995). Nowhere were the oppressive consequences of familial ideology more apparent than in legislation reinforcing the control of male employers over female domestic servants. As Judy Fudge indicates (this volume), the ideal of the benevolent father/employer was inscribed in the nineteenth century 'tort of seduction,' which awarded masters a monetary award for the seduction of formerly chaste female servants. Protective familial norms did not, however, extend to a legislated expectation that masters would provide benefits such as medical care to servants. The asymmetrical distribution of responsibilities and costs typical of contemporary employer-employee relations in private domestic service has clearly been established historically in law.

More recently, a federal government Conservative Party 'family caucus,' which existed for three years (1990 through 1992), was credited with policies that sought to impose on all Canadians a narrow, exclusive, sexist, heterosexual, and procreative family. The aim was to render invisible the circumstances of members of the household who were not part of a 'normal' family (i.e., two heterosexual parents and their children) (Freeman 1992, 42).[20] The mantra that domestic workers are 'one of the family' has repeatedly been invoked by state authorities whenever domestic workers have sought the protection of employment standards legislation. A clear instance of familial ideology was articulated by a member of the British Columbian Government Caucus in 1980 to rationalize the exclusion of live-in domestic workers from the BC Minimum Wage Act: 'Remember that a domestic has to be accepted into a family ... That is the reason a domestic cannot keep time. You are accepted into the family as part of the family, and the principle that you have your time recorded doesn't work in the family scene ...' (*BC Hansard*, 1980). The opposition by the Board of Trade of Metropolitan Toronto to exclusion of domestics from Ontario's collective bargaining legislation in 1993 similarly invoked the 'personal' and 'subjective' features of the employer-employee relationship in terms that might have been uttered a century ago (Judy Fudge, this volume).

Familial ideology masks the actual power relationship between employer and low-paid and vulnerable household employee. There are ambiguities within this ideology that encourage this process of masking, rendering the exploitive relationship less visible. One such ambiguity pertains to the distinction referred to above between the household, 'which may include kin and non-kin living in the same residence,' and the family, 'which refers ... to individuals related by blood ..., marriage, [or other "family-like" relations][21] whose relationships "transcend the residential unit"' (Strong-Boag 1985, 42). Acknowledging that domestic workers are members of the employer's household, but not members of the employer's family, might go a considerable distance in 'defamilializing,' and challenging, the arguments that have been used to deny domestic workers inclusion in labour legislation equal to other workers.

A second ambiguity in the use of familial ideology to oppress household workers is the definition by state authorities of the household as a 'private' realm and thus sheltered from state regulation. As Macklin (1994, 32) observes, 'Privileging a definition of the household as private, and thus immune from both market behaviour and state intervention, effectively effaces the domestic worker's identity as an employee in a workplace.' Labour gains for domestic workers would thus hinge not only on disentangling the two separate sets of relations pertaining to the family and the household respectively, but also on the insistence that the household can be a workplace, deserving of similar forms of protective state intervention as other workplaces. This means that domestic workers must be entitled to receive recognition that they are bona fide 'employees' under employment standards legislation. It would also entitle domestic employees to coverage equal to that of workers in the public sphere regarding maximum hours of work, overtime rates, statutory holiday provisions, and so on.

The ability to struggle successfully for decent working conditions and benefits is, as the authors in this book emphasize, significantly diminished as long as domestic workers are disenfranchised by the Canadian government through its immigration policy for migrant domestics. This denial of citizenship rights is supported with the added complicity of sending governments. For instance, as long as Canadian immigration policy (currently the LCP) makes it mandatory for migrant domestic workers to live in the household of their employers, they are denied what many domestics identify as the single most significant structural change in their circumstances: the right to live on one's own. The ability to shift from the dependency and indignity of living in the employer's home, to the relative autonomy and independence of day work is crucial to increasing the bargaining power of domestics in relation to their employers (Romero 1992, 63; Chaney and Castro 1989, 9; Glenn 1981).

Similarly, as long as migrant domestics are made vulnerable to threats of deportation by the absence of permanent legal status in the country, their ability individually or collectively to improve their conditions is greatly constrained. As Patricia Daenzer shows (this volume), the most recent reforms of the federal program for foreign domestics have done nothing to reverse this structural vulnerability. The stricter criteria for eligibility in the 1992 LCP has led to a drastic drop in the numbers of women admitted. The number of persons admitted to Canada through the LCP in 1995, for instance (1,866) is a little more than one-fifth of the number admitted in 1991 (8,630) (Canada, Citizenship and Immigration 1996). The increased difficulty of obtaining legal work as domestics undoubtedly leads to an increase in the number of migrant workers who work illegally. Those who have entered with visitor visas and then remain to work illegally in the country, or those who were refused refugee status, may be in the most vulnerable conditions as unprotected domestic employees. The current growth of a shadow market of undocumented workers means that a large number of domestics are finding themselves in even more precarious, coercive, and asymmetrical positions *vis-à-vis* employers and the state (Macklin 1992, 29–30). One of the key features of contemporary live-in domestic work which the editors address in Chapter One, is the unequal citizenship statuses between usually white, female, professional employers and predominantly immigrant Third World female employees.

Chapter Two by Sedef Arat-Koc provides a detailed historical overview of the treatment by the Canadian state and society of different racial/ethnic groups of foreign domestic workers. Although all foreign domestics have been subjected to restrictions over their personal freedoms, the harshest treatment has been reserved for women who were judged to be most distant from the ideal model of white British settler women. While British, and other white European women were welcomed as 'mothers of the nation,' women of colour from Third World countries were accepted only temporarily as expendable migrant labour and subjected to a high degree of political control.

In Chapter Three, Patricia Daenzer elaborates on the theme of the decline in rights of foreign domestics, which coincided with the shift to Third World sources such as the Caribbean and the Philippines. The reluctance of Canadian authorities to concede rights to Third World women migrants is apparent in the 'reforms' of the 1981 Foreign Domestic Movement and the 1992 Live-in Caregiver Program, which reinforce the unfree labour status of foreign domestics. Daenzer's analysis addresses the role of nation-to-nation relations in mediating restrictions on the freedoms of migrant household workers. The governments of sending states, which encourage the trade in female domestic labour as a means of alleviating chronic unemployment and balance of payment crises, are complicit in the exploitation and abuse of their nationals.

In Chapter Four, Judy Fudge highlights the role of organization, resistance, and the complexities of gaining meaningful reforms within private domestic service. Fudge shows how there is a wide juncture between formal equality attained through legal reform, such as inclusion within rights to collective bargaining, and substantive equality for domestic workers. The latter would entail the development of effective collective bargaining institutions and mechanisms. In fighting for collective bargaining rights for domestic workers, organizations such as INTERCEDE have engaged in important campaigns, challenging the ideologies associated with privacy, domesticity, and the sanctity of family that have permitted employers and the state to deny domestics the rights of other workers.[22] The pressure exerted by INTERCEDE and other groups has netted important symbolic victories, such as the inclusion of domestics in 1993 within Ontario's collective bargaining legislation. The focus of the ongoing struggle, however, has been to fashion effective democratic forms of representation that address the isolation and vulnerability of domestic working conditions. By 1996, the symbolic gains of domestic workers were reversed by the provincial Conservative government's sweeping labour legislation. Although these changes withdrew a large number of historic labour rights, this reversal reveals in particular how tenuous are the gains for a group of workers who are viewed as expendable non-citizen outsiders.

The accounts of their experiences by Miriam Elvir and Pura Velasco, two domestic worker activists who are survivors of the foreign domestic worker program in Canada, form the bases of Chapters Five and Six. Elvir and Velasco discuss the harsh political and economic conditions that prompted them to leave their home countries, their respective paths into foreign domestic service, the treatment they received from employers and immigration authorities, and their active participation in organizations seeking just and equitable conditions for domestic workers. Elvir recounts the indignities she suffered at the hands of wealthy employers, and the difficulties domestic workers from Third World countries typically encounter in receiving respect as workers and human beings. Velasco recounts the fear and intimidation instilled by the immigration regime that regulates foreign domestics. She forcefully argues that the vulnerability of foreign domestics would be considerably lessened if domestic employees were to have the same citizenship rights as their employers. Working to attain landed immigrant status for foreign domestics has been a central political goal for INTERCEDE, where Velasco served as president. Seeking justice for migrant workers through international solidarity is the central goal of the most recent organizing among activists such as Velasco.

Elvir and Velasco both emphasize the importance of the politicization, education, and organization by domestic workers themselves. For migrant women, domestic worker organizations offer a 'new family' where they find support and solidarity in dealing with recalcitrant employers, immigration authorities, and a variety of personal and legal difficulties (Chaney and Castro 1989, 10). Through the Montreal-based Association pour la Défense des Droits du Personnel Domestique, Elvir and other women are striving to negotiate better contracts for domestic workers through lobbying the Quebec government, and by running their own placement service. Velasco, who has worked in several countries, relates her recent experience in international organizing of domestics. Globally exploited, Filipino and other ethnic/national groups of migrant domestics are increasingly forging global links. One hundred and fifty domestics holding a candlelight vigil in Toronto for a slain sister in Singapore represent one ripple in a transnational movement to expose and challenge the injustices experienced by migrant domestic workers worldwide.

Notes

1 The alternative version of events believed by the Philippine public is that the Singaporean infant had accidentally drowned while bathing. Upon returning home and finding his son dead, the Singaporean father killed Ms Maga (*Sunday Morning*, CBC radio, 16 April 1995). While a Singaporean autopsy had originally led to a ruling that Ms Maga had died by strangulation, a second autopsy performed by a Philippine government medical examiner on the exhumed body four years later showed that she had been severely beaten, suggesting that the killer was much stronger than Ms Contemplacion and thus quite likely male. The Filipino investigators also found evidence on the body suggesting that the Singapore pathologists had 'tampered with the cadaver to simulate signs of strangulation' (Safire 1995).

2 The Philippine state has followed a two-pronged economic development strategy, supporting foreign and local investment in export processing zones (EPZs), and the export of labour. In the 1970s, contract migrant labour was predominantly male, travelling to the Middle East to work in construction, manufacturing, and technical services. The gender balance shifted in favour

of women migrants with the decline in industrial construction and the boom-induced expansion in household employment (Lycklama 1989, 35; Angeles 1993, 2). Contract migrant domestic workers and workers migrating from rural areas to take up work in the EPZs had much in common: their gender, migrant status, temporary work status, and conditions of restricted personal freedom (Gibson and Graham 1986, 144–5; Eviota 1990, 200).

3 Lee Kuan Yew was prime minister of Singapore for almost thirty years from independence to 1990. As First Minister, he continues to hold considerable power in the current government. His ruling People's Action Party has been careful to include members of minority ethnic communities and there is rather less discrimination against Malays and Indians in Singapore than there is discrimination against Chinese in Malaysia. We would like to thank Jeremy Paltiel for bringing this point to our attention.

4 Some Filipino domestics who became pregnant in Singapore were reported to have been forced by their employers to undergo abortions so as to continue employment and prevent forfeiting the mandatory bond of S$5,000 that employers must pay to ensure the 'good behaviour of migrants' (Medel-Anonueva, Abad-Sarmiento, and Oliveros-Vistro 1989, 166).

5 See Middle East Watch Women's Rights Project (1992) and the Philippines, Presidential Fact-Finding and Policy Advisory Commission On the Protection of Overseas Filipinos (Gancayco Commission) (1995), for a documented pattern of human-rights violations and extreme abuse of Asian maids in Kuwait and Saudi Arabia. Such abuse includes debt bondage, passport deprivation, forcible confinement, and isolation, as well as sexual, physical, and labour abuse.

6 Since the late 1980s, the Philippines has provided by far the largest source of those admitted into Canada's foreign domestic/live-in caregiver programs. For an analysis of some of the reasons for the regional and racial/ethnic sources of foreign domestic workers in Canada, see Bakan and Stasiulis (1995).

7 The waiting time for application for immigration to Canada is shorter in Hong Kong or Singapore than in Manila. Thus, out of the 6,000 Filipino domestics who came to Canada in 1989, only 1,500 passed through Manila (Bals 1990, 84).

8 In one reported case in London, Ontario, a domestic worker was kept imprisoned for three years in her employer's home and forbidden to have any outside contact, including use of the telephone or access to newspapers or television. Another case in London involved an African woman who was made to work in the employer's home in the day, and on a turkey farm at

night where her wages were pocketed by her employer ('Domestic Worker' 1992).

9 Terry Olayte, former nanny and organizer of the United Filipino Mothers' Association (Tesher 1995).

10 Certain structural trends have maintained a high level of demand for foreign domestic workers into the late twentieth century. These include the secular increase in labour force participation of (especially married) women, the unequal division of labour between men and women in the household, the critical shortage in licensed child care, and inadequacies in child-care subsidies, particularly felt by a large segment of middle-income earners. Key to the maintenance of high demand in household work, met by a supply of foreign, usually Third World women workers, are the intolerable working conditions associated with private domestic service (Bakan and Stasiulis 1995, 307–9).

11 In April 1995, sixty community-based organizations launched a constitutional challenge against the Ontario government, claiming it discriminates against Canadian-sponsored immigrants on welfare by providing them $100 a month less in welfare than other recipients. The rationale for the Ontario government's actions is that federal immigration policy makes the sponsors, rather than the government, responsible for the financial support of sponsored immigrants (Abbate 1995, A3B).

12 As Arat-Koc and Giles remark, 'In forms of reproductive and service work which take place in the public sphere, such as the fast-food industry and office or hotel cleaning, the employers are managers of large corporations and the relationships are impersonal and more fully commoditized than in private homes' (1994, 7).

13 For instance, Miriam Bals found in her interviews with twenty-two Filipino and twenty-two European domestics working in the wealthy municipality of Westmount, Quebec, that some of her respondents voiced that they felt they were 'a member of the family.' Some who felt this way further qualified this sentiment in stating that they were 'only a family member as long as they were needed' (Bals, 1990, 113).

14 In her interviews with twenty-five Chicana domestics in Denver, Colorado, Mary Romero found that 'only one domestic referred to her relationship with employers as "one of the family." All the other women retained a separation between tasks completed for their employers and "work of love" given to their families' (Romero 1992, 157).

15 This suggests that the redistribution of domestic work, including child care, can reasonably occur within the family. For many families (single-parent, dual-earning couples, elderly, people with disabilities, etc.), however, the

hiring of others to provide child care and assistance in household tasks may be a necessity.

16 Status differences through naming are reinforced by the linguistic practices of domestic placement agencies. In our study of domestic placement agencies in Toronto, we found that all of the agency owners interviewed routinely referred to domestic workers as 'girls,' while female employers were never referred to in this way (Bakan and Stasiulis 1995, 311, n.10). Colen found that West Indian domestic workers in New York found this asymmetry in address to be particularly offensive as the practice among all except intimates in their home cultures would be to address women as Miss or Mrs (1989, 182).

17 Heng and Devan argue that in Singapore, a separate, sexualized form of nationalism is advocated by state authorities for women and men. While men are expected to perform two and a half years of compulsory military service ('phallic nationalism'), educated Chinese women are exhorted to bear children as a form of National Service ('uterine nationalism'). As part of the Singaporean government's negative eugenics policy, Malay, Indian, and working-class women – i.e., those who are constructed in terms of reprobate ethnic, gender, and class stereotypes – are offered cash awards if they submit to tubal ligation and thereby restrict their childbearing to two children (Heng and Devan 1991, 346–7).

18 In a survey administered to 592 INTERCEDE members in 1990, '8.5 percent of the respondents said they felt the pressure to misrepresent themselves about marital status, and 5 percent about the presence of dependents' (Arat-Koc 1992, 242, n.9; Arat-Koc and Villasin 1990, 17).

19 Brigadier Yagoub al-Muhaini, director of Investigations, Ministry of Interior, Kuwait City, May 1992, quoted in Middle East Watch Women's Rights Project (1992, 6, emphasis added).

20 The caucus is credited with scrapping a long-term Conservative Party commitment to a national child-care program and introducing a targeted system of child benefits, which the caucus saw as encouraging women to stay at home (York 1992).

21 A variety of actually-existing families do not conform to the criteria of blood and marriage, including those composed of gays and lesbians, adoptive parents and children, unmarried people who do not meet common-law criteria and so on. For some creative discussions of 'who is family' and the implications of retaining or rejecting 'family status' in law, see Freeman (1992) and Gavigan (1992).

22 Shelley Gavigan points out that various 'de-familializing' campaigns engaged in by the women's and trade union movements have attempted to

undermine the oppressive consequences of familial ideology in law and social policy. These have included 'the struggle for universal child care, for women's access to safe birth control and legal abortion free from spousal hindrance, against family violence, for equal pay and employment equity, ... campaigns for full participation of the disabled in work and culture, and for protection and extension of universal health care' (1992, 33).

1

Foreign Domestic Worker Policy in Canada and the Social Boundaries of Modern Citizenship[1]

ABIGAIL B. BAKAN and DAIVA STASIULIS

Introduction: A Case Study of Non-Citizenship

Recent discussions in political philosophy have raised the thorny question of the rights associated with belonging to a particular political community, the nation-state, and the criteria used to define full and equal membership within this community (Balibar 1991; Fierlbeck 1991; Hall and Held 1989; Kymlicka 1995; Turner 1990; Young 1990). Several factors have renewed political and theoretical interest in questions of citizenship. These include dramatic shifts in global power and conflict over the reconfiguration of national boundaries associated with the end of the Cold War. Other factors are the emergence of new international patterns of production, and the consequent uneven development and displacement of peoples. In view of these global pressures, increasingly, states and communities are asking the question, 'To whom do we owe obligations and rights?'

Accompanying the increase in the volume and diversity of global migration has been an impulse within all countries in the northern hemisphere to limit the rights and obligations owed to 'outsiders,' including most critically the right to enter and to remain in a specific country (Yuval-Davis 1991, 61). This has been most dramatically expressed in the racist violence of far-right movements and political parties, which aim to turn back the clock on the reality of increasingly diverse racial and ethnic populations within the majority of most modern states. Definitions of citizenship conforming with traits associated with the race and ethnicity of dominant groups have also found support among politicians and parties of the left and centre, however.

More established citizens in advanced capitalist societies, experiencing increased levels of unemployment, deteriorating living standards, and a sense of powerlessness in the face of the restructuring strategies of international capital, are susceptible to claims that the shrinking privileges of citizenship in the 'developed' world must be 'protected' from 'aliens' – variously defined as immigrants, refugees, or Third World peoples (Richmond 1994).

While the so-called invasion of immigrants is the exaggerated rhetoric of politicians, the increase in global migration within and from Third World countries is real. This movement has included political refugees and others, euphemistically labelled 'economic refugees,' seeking means of individual and family survival (see Phizacklea 1983; Portes and Walton 1981; Sassen-Koob 1981; 1984).[2] In the early 1990s, informed estimates suggested that there were approximately 100 million migrants of all types, ranging from business migrants to illegal contract labourers, refugees, and asylum-seekers, who were working and living outside their countries of origin (Martin 1995, 821).[3] The acceleration and growing volume of this global migration is linked to contemporary changes in global capitalism, and the accompanying distorted development among Third World labour exporting regions (see Amin 1990; Cox 1991). The importance of international migration to sending countries is placed in perspective when one considers that labour is currently the second most important 'primary commodity' traded globally, the first being oil (Salt 1993, 1077).

Migratory movements from Third World to First World countries, as Robert Cox describes, have 'combined with the downgrading of job opportunities in advanced capitalist countries (the McDonaldization of the workforce) [to] constitute what has been called the "peripheralization of the core"'(1991, 340).[4] Within the growing sector of low-wage, unprotected jobs, the class division that defines a capitalist labour force has become further segmented by gender, race, and ethnicity. It has also been segmented by citizenship status, which, in turn, has governed access to a whole range of rights, including the protection of labour legislation.

One major, and growing, low-wage occupational sector, occupied in advanced capitalist countries mainly by Third World migrant women, is that of nannying or private domestic service. The state regulations governing foreign domestics vary from country to country. Generally, however, migrant domestic workers are assigned citizenship statuses subordinate to those of their citizen-employers. These may range from undocumented (or illegal) status, to indentured servitude or virtual slavery. As revealed in the January 1993 controversy over Zoe Baird, U.S. President Bill Clinton's first choice nominee for attorney general, the employment of illegal aliens as 'domestic help' is so widespread among affluent American families as to be generally merely 'winked at.'[5] In Canada, many Third World domestic workers endure a minimum of two years of virtual bonded servitude, institutionalized through the federal government's foreign domestic worker program. The major reason why the program continues to attract applicants despite these oppressive conditions is for 'a shot at the prize of landed immigrant [permanent resident] status' (Macklin 1992, 685).[6] In most First World countries, including Canada and the United States, the degraded legal statuses and conditions of foreign domestic workers have matured in a context of a general expansion of citizenship rights for immigrants and women. For this reason, the non-citizenship status of migrant female domestic workers has won notice for its 'anomalous,' 'paradoxical,' and 'anachronistic' character (see Arat-Koc 1989; Macklin 1992, 749).

This chapter explores the practices and relations of exclusion and inclusion at work within both the state and civil society, in constructing the social boundaries of citizenship. This is done by way of a case study, specifically the contemporary Canadian federal policy regarding the recruitment and regulation of foreign domestic workers. Our argument proceeds through the examination of the processes that construct one form of non-citizenship in Canada – corresponding to migrant domestic workers in the 'Foreign Domestic Movement' (FDM), renamed the 'Live-in Caregiver Program' (LCP) in April 1992. The FDM/LCP has existed since 1981 as a program of the Canadian federal government designed to facilitate the recruitment of thousands of migrant workers, the vast majority of whom are Third World women, to serve as live-in domestics and nannies for Canadian families.[7] This program, and the compulsory live-in, or indentured, status it entails, appear anomalous when viewed against the liberalization of Canadian immigration policy and general advances made by workers within the welfare state. Such advances include the post-war extension of legislative protection and collective bargaining rights for workers, and an increased recognition of gender- and race-based inequalities, formally reflected in the 1982 Canadian Charter of Rights and Freedoms, as well as in pay- and employment-equity legislation.[8] It is precisely the anomalous character of the FDM/LCP policy that we wish to reconsider.

The remainder of this chapter is organized into three sections. The first examines key features of Canadian government policies on foreign domestic workers that have led to a recent decline in citizenship rights for foreign domestics. This decline has coincided with the entry into this occupation of a significant number of Third World women of colour. The second section focuses on the types of social relations and accompanying discourses or rationales that reproduce the condition of bonded servitude inherent in the Canadian government's foreign domestic worker policies. The third and final section addresses the implications of the degraded legal and political status and social conditions of foreign domestic workers for a more generalized theory of citizenship. In the framework developed here, citizenship in any given country is to be understood as a variable and unequal process shaped not only by national/local conditions but also by global realities and accompanying racialized, gendered discourses. Such a perspective challenges traditional approaches to citizenship that assume a single, advanced nation-state model, from which the attainment of rights is inappropriately universalized.

The Canadian Foreign Domestic Movement/Live-in Caregiver Program (FDM/LCP): The Construction of an Anomaly

Prior to World War Two, theories of eugenics helped shape the project of nation-building in Canada through the incorporation of ideas about the superiority of the 'Anglo-Saxon' race, and race-specific notions of womanhood in immigration policy, reproductive policies, public health, and education (McLaren 1990; Stasiulis and Williams 1992). Canada's vision of its place in the world, until at least World War Two, coincided with the global dimensions of the British Empire. This was reflected in Canada's citizenship laws, which, prior to 1947, defined Canadian nationals not as 'Canadian citizens' but as 'British subjects,' both in Canada and abroad. A racial/ethnic hierarchy in immigration policy emerged that judged potential migrants according to their distance from, or proximity to, 'white British' ideals.

In the pre-war years, the major sources of foreign domestics were the United Kingdom and Western Europe. The majority of these European domestics entered with landed immigrant status, or with less restrictive conditions than those governing the eligibility for permanent residence of contemporary migrant domestics. Between the 1890s and the 1920s, the young women recruited as domestics predominantly from Great

Britain were granted landed immigrant status on the stipulation that they would provide live-in service for six months. English and Scottish 'girls' were sought by British-Canadian families to meet the demand for domestic workers. As in other 'white settler colonies,' such immigration was seen to play an explicit nation-building role: white British domestics were chosen with an eye toward their future role as wives and mothers (Abele and Stasiulis 1989; Stasiulis and Jhappan 1995; DeVan 1989, 35; Barber 1986b; Arat-Koc this volume).

During the Second World War, Canadian authorities capitalized on the vulnerability of East European refugees, considered to be less ethnically 'desirable' than British domestics. Among the 'DP' (Displaced Persons) labour, invidious distinctions were made based on ethnicity and religion, with preference given to applicants of Baltic origin and to Protestants (Danys 1986, 133–4). These displaced persons were indentured as domestics to Canadian families for a period of one year. The continued labour shortage of domestics prompted the Canadian government in the early 1950s to establish special group movements (permitted only by Order-in-Council) of German, and then Italian and Greek, domestics, who were, in contrast to British domestics, subjected to unusual scrutiny and the suspicious attitudes of immigration authorities (Daenzer 1991, 123–6). In theory, however, all European domestics shared the unconditional right of residency in Canada, having entered Canada with the legal status of landed immigrants (Daenzer 1991, 127).

The most restrictive and coercive policies were reserved for Third World women of colour. Like other Caribbean blacks, female domestics were excluded from Canadian immigration on the basis of their supposed inability to adapt to the Canadian climate, and their assumed sexual licentiousness (Calliste 1993/4; MacKenzie 1988; Timoll 1989, 38–9). Following a one-time experiment in 1910–11, when a small group of domestics were brought to Canada from Guadeloupe, this exclusion lasted until 1955. In June of that year, the Canadian cabinet finally approved admission of 100 'coloured' women from the British West Indies. This 'gesture of goodwill' was a deliberate effort on the part of the Canadian Government to maintain Canada's preferential trade and investment position in the British Caribbean (Calliste 1989, 133; 1993/4).

While black domestics were formally granted the right to full landed status upon arrival, this right was compromised by an unusual agreement signed with the two Caribbean nations (Jamaica and Barbados) concerned. This agreement stipulated that should the women be found unsuitable for domestic work, they would be returned to their country of origin at the expense of the Caribbean government. Black women were also subjected to the indignity of medical testing for venereal disease, revealing Canadian authorities' racist attitudes about the suggested promiscuity of black women. In a pattern that would become familiar to all domestics from Third World countries, the harsh and unequal treatment of Caribbean domestics in Canada went unchallenged by the governments of the Caribbean nations, which encouraged emigration as a means of alleviating conditions of chronic unemployment (Calliste 1989, 143; Daenzer this volume).

With the introduction by the Canadian federal government in 1973 of the Temporary Employment Authorization Program, domestic workers received short-term work permits, thus replacing the previous scheme's provision of permanent resident status upon arrival. These women were permitted to stay in Canada conditional upon the performance of domestic work for a designated employer, thus transforming 'domestic workers into ... disposable migrant labourers, not unlike European "guest workers"' (Macklin 1992, 691). During the 1970s, the citizenship rights of foreign, and especially Caribbean, domestics thus deteriorated further. While many European domestics continued to enter Canada as landed immigrants, Caribbean domestics increasingly entered on temporary employment visas, which gave maximum control to the state and employers over the conditions of work and residence of women of colour domestics.

Entry under temporary employment visas placed domestics in an ambiguous, 'technically non-existent' immigration category of 'visiting immigrant' bearing 'the burdens of both immigrants and visitors, yet [receiving] the benefits of neither' (Macklin 1992, 697–8). In practice, migrant domestics have endured restrictions in freedoms generally considered unacceptable, and rejected by other workers, in liberal democracies. Because of the popular purchase of racist and sexist assumptions shaping dominant notions of who is and who is not legitimately a Canadian, however, which is consistent with the 'nation-building' ideology of earlier decades, what is unacceptable for most was rendered acceptable for designated 'others,' notably non-citizen women of colour.

The Canadian government's objective of bringing in domestic workers under temporary work permits was transparent: to create an indentured or captive labour force, at low cost to the Canadian government, who were unlikely to quit regardless of how exploited their work and living situations.[9] In 1981, a revised policy, the Foreign Domestic Movement (FDM), was introduced that further institutionalized this objective, while providing migrant domestics the chance for improved citizenship status in the future. Under this program, a foreign domestic worker was eligible to apply for landed immigrant status after two years of live-in service with a designated employer. Employers could only be changed with the approval of a federal immigration officer. If the worker successfully achieved landed status, all of the restrictions associated with the FDM ceased to apply, and access to all formal rights open to permanent residents could be obtained. However, if after three assessments the domestic worker had not been accepted for permanent resident status, she would have to return to her country of origin. The alternative would be to remain illegally in Canada and to work in the shadow economy, an option which appears to have become more common among foreign domestics since the introduction of the new stringent admissions criteria.[10]

Until January 1992, when the Minister for Immigration announced policy changes to the FDM, eligibility for landed status in Canada hinged not only on two years of continuous service as live-in domestics, but also upon the meeting of specific requirements to prove 'self-sufficiency.' These included evidence of occupational upgrading, 'social adaptation' to the community and public life in Canada through the performance of volunteer work, and 'financial security' as reflected in savings from domestic workers' meagre earnings. These criteria were regarded as grossly unfair by domestics and their advocates, especially as they were not used to assess the suitability for landing of any other group of immigrants whose occupations, like those of domestic workers, were in high demand in Canada (Arat-Koc 1991, 8).

Under the 1992 guidelines for the new Live-in Caregiver Program, the upgrading requirements were eliminated in assessments for landed status for foreign domestics, who were now called 'caregivers.' Eligibility criteria for entry into Canada by migrant caregivers became more restrictive, however. The revised Live-in Caregiver Program initially called for the completion of the equivalent of a Canadian grade twelve education, and six months of full-time formal training in a field or occupation related to the job sought in Canada as live-in caregiver. The reasons given by the Immigration Department for upgrading the admissions criteria for foreign domestics were, first, the perceived need to improve the quality of childcare, and second, to facilitate the entry into the larger labour market of those domestics who have attained landed status. In June 1993, the Immigration Department bowed to mounting pressures to rescind the new training criterion by agreeing to allow applicants to substitute twelve months of practical experience for the six-month training announced in April 1992 ('Ottawa Revises' 1993). The experience criteria are still fairly narrowly defined, however, so that the applicant must have gained the experience in the last three years from application, and must have had at least six months continuous experience with one employer (Interview with Linda MacDougall, 2 May 1996).

The two most repressive aspects of the Foreign Domestic Movement regulations have been retained under the Live-in Caregiver Program, in spite of the government's attempt to sell the new program through the rhetoric of 'reform' resulting from 'widespread consultation.'[11] These are: the temporary migrant or 'visitor' status; and the compulsory live-in requirement for foreign domestic workers. The anomalous character of the FDM/LCP is reflected in the historical reversal in one of the most basic of rights previously enjoyed by foreign domestics, notably 'the right to enter, and once having entered, the right to remain in a specific country' (Yuval-Davis 1991, 61). This reversal in the accessibility of female domestics to permanent residence in Canada coincided with the relative increase in the number of domestics recruited from Third World sources, who were also women of colour.

The historic decline in foreign domestics' access to permanent residency, which occurred with the transition from landed status to employment visas, was accompanied by another major restriction – the entrenchment in the policy of a mandatory live-in requirement for all participants in the FDM. Early domestic employment agreements, such as those composed by the minister of Labour in the 1940s, omitted reference to live-in arrangements. While the majority of domestic workers lived in the homes of their employers, not all did, nor was it mandatory (Daenzer 1991, 152). The live-in condition of foreign domestics became mandatory in the 1981 regulations that specified that 'only live-in domestics are eligible for consideration under the FDM.' The 1992 changes in the regulations governing entry of foreign domestics under the LCP restated that the purpose of the policy is solely to bring in live-in domestics, based on the argument that jobs for live-out service can be readily filled by workers in the Canadian labour market.

Domestic workers are highly vulnerable to abusive conditions as a result of the live-in requirement and the ambiguity of the social space constructed out of relations between live-in domestic workers and their employers. A 'dialectic of intimacy and domination' is rooted in the contradictions that exist between the status of domestic work as wage labour in the cash nexus, and its highly personalized nature and location in the private household (Romero 1992, 136; see also Bakan and Stasiulis, Introduction; Macklin 1992, 728; Rollins 1985). Exploitation of live-in domestic workers may arise almost invisibly, as there is an inherent expectation of the offer of 'sacrifices' associated with 'family ideology' – sacrifices of time, privacy, energy, and so on. Privacy and 'time off' are frequently non-existent for domestic workers who live with their employers, and who may be on call twenty-four hours a day.[12] Waged domestic workers are commonly expected to offer their time and services out of goodwill to their employing families in ways that would be unthinkable in most public employment situations in an advanced capitalist state. Domestic workers are reticent to attempt to escape such imposition, however, because of their requisite live-in status and the perpetual threat of deportation associated with workplace conflict or employer reprisals. Susceptibility to sexual, physical, and emotional abuse and racial harassment by employers and other household members, and by friends of the employing family, are also heightened by living in the employer's household (Cohen 1987; Silvera 1983).

Not all live-in domestic employment situations are, of course, abusive, nor does our argument rest on the claim that they inevitably are so. The essential point is that whether abuse does or does not take place has an accidental character, subject to the individual conditions of work of the live-in domestic, and the individual attitudes, perceptions, or even mood-swings of the employing family. The Canadian government, in its booklet on the LCP for employers and live-in caregivers, now acknowledges the existence of abuse (Canada, Citizenship and Immigration 1993, 7). The two features defining the inherently unfree status of the foreign domestic worker – the compulsory live-in requirement and the precarious immigration status – together leave the domestic worker with few resources to resist demeaning and threatening treatment by employers.

These features are structural, as well as embedded into the very definition of Canadian citizenship rights, including the conditional restriction of those rights to non-citizens. Legal protection for wages and working conditions and the practical access to avenues of protection are minimal for foreign domestics. The eligibility requirements and the general practices involved in foreign domestic employment are regulated by a federal agreement administered by the Employment and Immigration Commission. Yet the employer/employee agreement is not a legal contract, nor has its enforceability ever been subject to court challenge

(Canada, Citizenship and Immigration 1993, 5; Bretl and Davidson 1989, 3; Macklin 1992, 722–3). Additional regulations applicable to domestic workers exist under the jurisdiction of the provinces. However, provincial labour standards for domestics vary from one province of Canada to another and are invariably substandard in comparison with those that apply to other categories of workers (West Coast Domestic Workers Association 1989; Conseil des Communautes culturelles et de l'immigration 1992; Fudge this volume).

Despite these barriers, domestic workers have not been silent or passive. While individually vulnerable through the Canadian state's denial of civil and political rights and the constant threat of deportation, collectively domestic workers have successfully contested some of the terms and conditions of their oppression. The vigorous lobbying efforts of such grass roots organizations as INTERCEDE[13] in Toronto culminated in the revision to the 1981 Temporary Employment Authorization Program, enabling foreign domestics to apply for landed status while remaining in Canada after two years of live-in service. Further, during the late 1970s, faced by increasing pressures for reform by domestic advocacy groups, the federal government included domestic workers in the Unemployment Insurance and Canada Pension Plans. However, the extension of such select labour rights to domestic workers has not represented an unqualified gain for those on temporary visas insofar as entitlement has explicitly been tied to citizenship. Thus, domestic workers are discouraged from collecting unemployment insurance while on temporary visas because, by definition, they are not expected to be unemployed while staying in the country.[14] Similarly, while Canada Pension Plan contributions may be regained, the process is difficult and time-consuming, thus limiting the number of people who have attempted to collect (DeVan 1989, 67).

Most recently, the April 1992 changes in foreign domestic policy, repackaged as the Live-in Caregiver Program, were met by a storm of protest by domestic advocacy groups. The LCP was widely viewed as a policy instrument designed to drastically reduce the number of nannies from the major Third World source regions of domestics currently employed in Canada. Domestic advocacy groups and legal advisers have maintained that the policy is racist insofar as it disqualifies many domestic workers from Third World countries who are unable to meet the increased educational and training requirements (Canadian Advisory Council on the Status of Women, 1 February 1992). The fears of these groups have been borne out in recent statistics, revealing that

while the percentage of entrants into the LCP from the Phili
remained high (61 per cent in 1992 and 1994, 75 per cent in
overall numbers of domestics entering under the LCP have been drastically reduced (Mitchell 1993). Thus, the number of entrants into the LCP
in 1995 (1,866) was just over one fifth of the entrants into the 1991 FDM
(8,630) and only 17 per cent of the 1990 figure (10,739). According to a
senior policy advisor in Citizenship and Immigration Canada, about
2,000 authorizations are likely to be issued through the LCP in 1996
(Interview with Linda MacDougall, 2 May 1996). This precipitous drop
in numbers of migrants through the LCP has closed off an important
source for legal entry and acquisition of Canadian residence and citizenship for Third World women. The increased difficulty of working legally
as foreign domestics undoubtedly leads to an increase in the number of
migrant workers whose worker status is undocumented, such as those
who enter with visitor or student visas and remain to work illegally in
the country.

In sum, the case that the FDM/LCP is an anomalous instance of non-
citizenship is maintained because it has matured in a general context of
postwar expansion of citizenship rights and 'liberalization' of immigration policy, in Canada specifically and Western, industrialized countries
more generally. The unique restrictions on foreign domestic workers are
apparent in the particular intersection of the absence of rights attached
to the temporary work visa on the one hand, and the mandatory live-in
requirement on the other. The anomalous features of the foreign domestic program do not, however, mean that it is a racist and sexist policy in
contrast to other Canadian policy areas that are impartial, fair, and universal. Rather, it is anomalous only in the degree of its transparency,
revealing ideological and institutionalized processes that are more commonly hidden.

Global Relations and Racialization in First World Households

The fact that Third World female migrants have rights that are relin-
quished upon migration to Canada is consistently ignored by immigration officials, employers, and scholars of citizenship, who focus only
on the gains that migration confers upon those arriving from underdeveloped regions. For instance, immigration authorities, placement
agencies, and state 'femocrats' (whose constituency is more likely to be
the employers of domestics than the domestics themselves) have all

portrayed Third World migrant women entering through foreign domestic policy as beneficiaries of foreign aid (Arat-Koc 1992). The gains of First World citizenship are, moreover, not assured for foreign domestics on temporary work visas, who win only the right to apply for landed status in exchange for two years of virtually indentured service.

The socio-political construction of the 'foreign domestic worker' replicates within Canada elements of the unequal and exploitative features of global relations between developed and underdeveloped states. Ideologies associated with 'domestic labour,' 'the family,' and the distinction between the 'private' and the 'public' are both racialized and gendered. Such ideologies aid in the recreation, in microcosm, within the private Canadian home, of the hegemonic relationship of Canada to the domestic worker's Third World home country.

In the process of entering Canada to perform domestic labour for a Canadian family, the 'foreign domestic worker' is socially and politically constructed to provide a waged substitute for the unpaid labour otherwise performed by a Canadian woman. The availability of labour for this form of employment in Third World countries is a direct result of a dependent type of capitalism that produces markedly uneven development. In postcolonial conditions, the legacy of imperialism in the Third World has combined with modern conditions of indebtedness to generate large pools of female migrant labour to fill the demand in the domestic care industry of industrially advanced states. Global conditions of recession have created increased pressures for qualified applicants from Third World countries to attempt to enter more advanced states under any terms, even if this involves considerable deskilling in employment (Bakan 1987). Landlessness, poverty, and unemployment have been exacerbated by structural adjustment policies implemented by national political and landed elites working together with the World Bank and International Monetary Fund in the wake of the debt crises. These pressures are intensified by highly indebted governments of developing countries, which come to regard receipt of migrants' remittances as central pillars of their economies, giving them a clear interest in promoting labour export. In Canada, the two major Third World source regions of foreign domestics have been the English Caribbean and the Philippines. This migratory relationship is directly linked to the conditions of underdevelopment within these regions (Bakan and Stasiulis 1995, 315–17; 1996).

While poverty and underdevelopment have manufactured the supply of migrant female labour, the availability of live-in domestic employment in countries such as Canada has been a direct product of the expansion of employment options for women in advanced capitalist states. Even in periods of high unemployment, when demand for domestic workers would logically be dampened, such demand has tended to remain high (Scane and Holt 1988, 28; Timoll 1989, 4).[15] With increasing employment of women outside the home, and the growing dependence of family earnings upon two adult incomes, what has been described as the 'crisis in the domestic sphere' has increased (Arat-Koc 1989, 34ff). The critical shortage in child care, and the high costs of regulated public child care, render the decision among Canadian families to hire a live-in foreign domestic a choice taken within a context of limited options. The continued reality for most women is that responsibility for domestic labour falls squarely on their shoulders. Conditions of poverty and repression in Third World countries, however, combine with restrictive immigration policies of advanced states to provide a captive pool of low-wage labour for live-in service. In such conditions, the feelings of guilt and ambivalence of the women in the First World household who can afford a private solution to the domestic crisis may give way to a sense of relief.[16]

In the process of hiring a foreign domestic, what can be abstractly referred to as the Canadian family 'home' is itself transformed. In fact, what occurs is a series of simultaneous transformations, all mediated by the wider global relations 'lived' within a single household. Rather than being a social space apart from the workplace, the home in which a foreign domestic worker is employed is transformed, partially, into a workplace. This transformation of social space also applies to those who take on the role of 'employer.' In addition to the roles of 'mother,' 'spouse,' and 'member of the family,' there is also the social construction of the 'boss.' The 'private' domicile is therefore rendered, again partially and ambiguously, into a public domain. Although it remains a private family dwelling, it also becomes subsumed under the direction of public state legislation. As such, it is subject, again partially and ambiguously, to formal and informal regulations applicable to a public business and work environment.

The domestic employee is also transformed in the process of her simultaneous entry into Canada, and into the Canadian home as a place of work. The household worker is a member of an alternative family unit and her own network of kin and support relations. She may herself be a mother and/or a spouse upon her arrival to Canada. The FDM/LCP regulations compel the disaggregation of that family, and curtail the freedom of association of the employee to form a future family, or family-like relations. The effect of the Canadian foreign domestic policy has consistently been to 'conceal marital and family commitments' of foreign domestics (Macklin 1992, 734–8). This occurred first by disqualifying women who were married or had dependent children, and more recently, by continuing to use marital and family status as criteria in the initial selection process of foreign caregivers.

Another transformation that occurs upon the employment of a foreign domestic is the entry of her household unit into the cash nexus of advanced capitalist social relations. A percentage of the wages of the foreign domestic worker is usually sent back to the employee's family in the home country. Remittances have increasingly become part of a general strategy for Third World families' survival and advancement (Mitter 1986, 37; Deere et al. 1990).[17] The perception that even the lowest wages in the most undesirable type of work in Canada are still preferable to those available in the home country is a powerful incentive compelling the foreign domestic worker to accept such employment (DeVan 1989, 82; Trager 1984; Silvera 1989).

The ambiguity of the social space constructed out of relations between live-in domestic workers and their employers creates complex and contradictory interests and expectations, including contested, and cross-cultural, assumptions about appropriate roles and behavior related to 'family life.' The unequal status of employer and employee, simultaneously a relationship between 'citizen' and 'non-citizen,' renders such relations inherently reflective of the uneven relationship between the states of origin of the two parties.

The highly unequal citizenship statuses of the domestic worker and her employer are rendered even more complex by the racial/ethnic differentiation involved in the transformation of the home into a workplace for foreign domestics. Here, again, there are many possible variations. The 'foreign' factor in the social construction of the foreign domestic worker assumes an element of 'sameness' among the 'others' as non-Canadian. Because the employment locus is the private home, however, and usually involves the hiring by the employer of a single employee, the process of selection becomes highly sensitive to factors and stereotypes associated with the country of origin of the prospective domestic employee.

The racialization of relations between employer and domestic worker does not happen naturally or automatically, but is a socially and politically constructed process mediated by a variety of 'gatekeepers.' The mediating role of gatekeepers is endemic to this constructive process. The gatekeepers include the governments and state agencies in both sending and receiving countries, private domestic recruitment and placement agencies, government visa officers and other immigration personnel. In the past, Caribbean governments were key agents in the Caribbean Domestic Scheme, instituting 'a rigorous selection process to ensure that candidates for the Domestic Scheme would establish a good name for Caribbean people' (Calliste 1989, 143). Currently, the mediating role of private domestic placement agencies is central to the social construction and regulation of the foreign domestic worker program (Bakan and Stasiulis 1995).[18] The success of a given domestic placement business often depends upon the offer of a 'guarantee,' i.e., a commitment to replace the domestic worker if the the 'match' is not satisfactory (*'Matchmaking Tips'* 1989, 1–3). The industry is therefore highly sensitized to personal and 'private' criteria for hiring in the home, criteria that are not generally formally or legally acceptable in a publicly regulated employment process.

In practice, the work of gatekeepers such as domestic placement agencies is accomplished through the construction, articulation and reproduction of stereotypes about who is, or is not an appropriate caregiver for 'Canadian' families.[19] Such stereotypes are also operative in assessing the appropriate candidates for future citizenship within advanced nation states. During the 1950s and 1960s, the prevalent image of Caribbean nannies was that of the obliging and loving 'mammy' (Calliste 1989, 144). The shift in primary sources of foreign domestics to Canada from the Caribbean to the Philippines that occurred in the 1980s is in part explained by the debasement undergone in the image of West Indian 'island girls' and the emergence of images of Filipino nannies as 'naturally' nurturing, docile, and 'good with children' (Bakan and Stasiulis 1995; Macklin 1992, 700–1). The racialized images of the domesticity of different national groups of women are variable and subject to reversal, indicated when formerly 'submissive' domestics begin to organize and assert their rights. Thus, militant organizing for domestic workers' rights has not been consistent with either the historic 'mammy' stereotype or the image of the docile and loyal Filipina, leading to alteration and qualification in marketable stereotypes (Bakan and Stasiulis 1995, 322).

Exploitation within foreign domestic service is inherent in the constraints of precarious immigration status and the requirement to live in the employer's home, rather than in the race/ethnicity of employers and employees. Nonetheless, racism deepens and provides additional ideological justification for such exploitation. In view of the shared gender of employers and employees, racialized images of womanhood play an important role in justifying to employers why non-white women of colour are 'naturally' suited for childcare and housework.[20] However, the most significant sources for the racial/ethnic variations in the degree of exploitation experienced by foreign domestics reside not in racial/gendered stereotypes, but rather in the different citizenship statuses and motivations of white/European vs. Third World women of colour.[21] Foreign domestic workers who originate from Britain or France generally do not experience, nor would they normally tolerate, the range of abuses suffered by foreign domestics from the Caribbean or the Philippines. A much smaller proportion of women from Europe enter into the FDM or LCP in order to gain permanent residence in Canada (Interview with Linda MacDougall, 2 May 1996).[22] The threat of deportation to a more affluent European country does not hold the same implications as it does to a poor Third World country.

Viewing Citizenship Globally

This chapter began with the observation that in conditions of global recession and instability, the powers of First World states are increasingly being used to police and limit access of Third World migrants to rights associated with First World citizenship. Such policing is evident in Canadian policies regulating foreign domestic workers, particularly as they have been applied to Third World women of colour.

Foreign domestic workers are only one of several categories of migrants in Canada and other developed countries who are disadvantageously being incorporated within hierarchies of citizenship.[23] Such matching of positions within racial/ethnic and gender relations to degrees of citizenship rights suggests the need to revise theories of citizenship that view the latter as hinged only to 'universal' or achievement-based attributes. To understand citizenship, and the boundaries drawn between citizenship and non-citizenship, a reconceptualization is necessary that views citizenship as a dynamic rather than a static process. This process can be seen to draw upon particularistic criteria (race, ethnicity, gender) that simultaneously reflect both global and national relations of power.

Previous efforts to understand the anomalous character of the FDM/

LCP, for example, reveal how it reflects an intersection of racial, gender, and class structures and biases at work at the level of discourse, state policy, bureaucratic relations, and regulations with civil society (Arat-Koc 1989; 1991; Enloe 1989; Calliste 1989; Cohen 1987; Macklin 1992; Timoll 1989). Such explanations for the subordinate legal-juridical position of foreign domestics are partial and incomplete. Thus, while citizenship differences among women are featured in some analyses of the oppression of foreign domestic workers, citizenship becomes merely one of several dichotomous variables including those of gender, race, and class that 'legitimate inferior conditions and lesser rights' (Arat-Koc 1989, 48) for those who fall on the wrong side of the dichotomy (see also Macklin 1992, 686, 752). The fact that 'non-citizenship' is assumed to be an intrinsic aspect of foreign domestic worker policy has the effect of concealing the dynamics underlying the construction of boundaries between 'citizens' and 'non-citizens.' With few exceptions of analyses that take into consideration the effects of underdevelopment and international debt politics in Third World countries in motivating women to take up domestic jobs overseas (see especially Calliste 1989; Macklin 1992, 694–6), most accounts lack a more general consideration of the global context in which citizenship statuses for Third World migrants in First World states are negotiated. For Third World women, entry into Canada as foreign domestic workers has always involved some trade-off between Third World and First World citizenship (Calliste 1989, 143).

Traditional models of citizenship generally either accept or amend T.H. Marshall's evolutionary perspective, where citizenship rights are treated as the imminent effect of the development of Western societies. Such understandings of citizenship are ill-equipped to deal with the growing reality of non-citizens such as foreign domestic workers (Layton-Henry 1990; Soysal 1994). For the Third World non-citizen in search of First World citizenship, gaining access to social rights – particularly 'the right to a modicum of economic welfare and security' (Marshall 1950, 78) – commonly supersedes entry to civil and political rights. Thus, to gain certain social rights such as access to adequate health and educational services, citizens of the Philippines or Jamaica exit their home countries, and in so doing, forfeit a range of regionally and nationally defined civil, political, social, and cultural rights. These forfeited rights may include the rights of land ownership, associated with citizenship and residence in less developed countries.[24] They also give up certain social rights, such as the right to live with one's children and other family members, the right to freedom of choice of domicile, and access to networks of support in the provision of health care, child care, food, and so on.

State regulations restricting the rights and freedoms of migrants imposed by both 'host' and 'sending' governments reflect unequal relations between First World and Third World countries. A recognition of the capacity of more advanced states to carry out actions beneficial to its citizens and prejudicial to migrants from Third World states, and which are thereby successful in pitting the strategic interests of citizens against non-citizens, is integral to this approach.[25] The acceptance of the regulatory authority of hegemonic states in determining access to citizenship rights is not only reflected in the racialized and gendered definition of who is and who is not suitable to obtain such rights. It is also apparent in the assumption of the permanently subordinate status of Third World states.

The structural unevenness in the global political economy lends itself to a notional hierarchy of citizenship rights on an international scale. Advanced western liberal democracies, where the economies are more industrially developed and welfare states are established, appear to offer a potential 'pool' of citizenship rights that is significantly greater than those on offer to the vast majority who live in Third World nations. The appearance of such a pool of rights, regardless of the restrictive conditions assigned to their acquisition, is in sharp contrast to the potential pool available in conditions of chronic underdevelopment. Moreover, the unequal distribution of citizenship rights within the advanced liberal democracies, principally along the lines of class, race, and gender inequalities, recedes in importance when counterposed to societies where the vast majority of citizens suffer from chronic poverty and privation.

Marshall's notion of the emergence of citizenship as a process of institutionally regulated civil, political, and social rights may be recast in light of such a globalized conceptual model. Marshall's definition of citizenship was intrinsically linked to the notion of modernization, with the advanced capitalist state as a central focal point for the development of his conceptual model. Such a universalization is, however, misplaced. The process of migration from a Third World state, and entry into an advanced, or globally hegemonic, state, usually entails the loss of certain citizenship rights that migrants enjoyed in their home countries. The 'gains' may be measured more as economic opportunities rather than rights, the losses measured more in political, cultural, and social terms – all of which are underlined by the fact that the increases in economic well-being are extended on a limited and retractable basis, not as inviolate rights, which can be achieved only in the presence of full political equality.

The process of entering an advanced state (for any purpose other than tourism) is highly controlled, and one over which the non-citizen migrant has no formal rights. The 'right to enter a country of one's choice' is contradictory to the very idea of citizenship in common Western liberal discourse. The method of entry – legal or illegal, as a refugee fleeing from a state, as a prospective employee destined to fill a perceived labour market demand in the host state, or as an investor immigrant promising to bring in large amounts of capital, as a lone individual or as a member of a family or network, and so on – is therefore critical to the achievement of citizenship rights upon entry. The terms of entry are set primarily by the receiving state (although regulations established by the sending state may also play a role), and such terms interact with several sets of labour, social welfare, and human rights laws in the receiving state to affect the economic, social, and political well-being of migrants and their families.

Further, hegemonic states, and other gatekeeping agents in civil society working in such policy areas as immigration, labour market and social welfare, play a central role in mediating the contact between the non-citizen and the citizen. They also play a role in ensuring the reproduction of these relationships along racially and ethnically segmented lines, in accordance with broader patterns of global inequities. The assumption of an international system of hegemonic and non-hegemonic states, where the latter are treated a priori to be inferior in terms of access to democratic rights, economic opportunities, and freedoms becomes embodied in the citizenship status of the individual Third World migrant.

When that individual migrant is also a woman and/or a person of colour, further discriminatory factors characteristic of citizenship rights within the hegemonic state itself – i.e., sexism and racism – amplify the restrictions to citizenship rights of the migrant non-citizen. Central also to the structure and process of this mediation are the gendered discourses and practices that define, and socially construct, boundaries between the 'public' and the 'private' spheres for citizens and non-citizens alike. These processes operate in combination to ensure and regulate a series of mutually reinforcing gendered and racialized discourses pertaining to nationhood and citizenship that define the boundaries between 'citizens' and excluded 'others.' Citizenship, both in advanced capitalist states and in states with histories of conquest and colonialism, is thus crucially inscribed by global relations of inequality.

Observers' Notes and Interviews

Canadian Advisory Council on the Status of Women, 1 February 1992. Meeting convened with domestic workers groups to discuss changes in the regulations of the Foreign Domestic Movement program, Ottawa, observers' notes by Daiva Stasiulis.

Interview (by Daiva Stasiulis) with Linda MacDougall, Senior Policy Advisor, Citizenship and Immigration Canada, Ottawa, 2 May 1996.

Notes

1 This paper is part of a larger study entitled 'Women of Colour, Work and Citizenship: Filipino and West Indian Domestic Workers and Registered Nurses in Toronto,' directed by the authors and supported by the Social Sciences and Humanities Research Council of Canada and the Advisory Research Council of Queen's University. It is a revised and updated version of an earlier article (Bakan and Stasiulis 1994). We would like to thank Judith Adler Hellman, Sedef Arat-Koc, George Dei, Patricia Daenzer, Radha Jhappan, Catherine LaGrande, Stephen Newman, and George Stubos for their helpful comments on an earlier draft of this paper, and Leonora Angeles for her expert research assistance. Previous versions were presented to the Groupe de recherche ethnicité et societés (GRES) at the University of Montreal (October 1992), and the Feminist Legal Workshop at the University of Toronto Law School (March 1993).

2 The current number of refugees worldwide (as defined by the UN Convention) was estimated in 1991 to be about 20 million, more than double the number in 1980. An additional 20 million people are estimated to be displaced within the borders of their own countries (Brazeau 1992, ix; Elliot and Fleras 1992, 244). Of course, migration within and from Third World countries is not the only type of contemporary international migration. There has also been a real increase in migration within and between advanced capitalist nation states. The reorganization of global capitalism has also led to a rise in the migration of professional, technical, and managerial labour.

3 According to Martin (1995, 821), this estimate excludes tourists and other temporary visitors. Anthony Richmond (1994, xi) cites a lower estimate of 70 million migrants, with more than one million emigrating permanently every year.

4 Our use of such terms as 'First World,' 'Third World,' 'advanced,' 'developing,' 'hegemonic,' etc., to designate the economic status of given states in the global economy in no way accepts that these states can be ranked according to ethical or cultural criteria. Nor do we accept a static evolutionary schema of development with 'developed' or 'advanced' states at the pinnacle. While we recognize some of the problems of interpretation in retaining these terms, we continue to employ them in the absence of ready alternatives, and with the understanding that the development of developing states has been blocked as a result of their relations with developed, imperialist states. We conceive of the global system of hegemonic and non-hegemonic states as a spectrum of intersecting relationships in an international division of labour. For an interesting critique of the racialized connotations of the three world division see Goldberg (1993, 163–8).

5 Following her disclosure that she had knowingly hired two undocumented workers from Peru as domestic workers, Zoe Baird withdrew her nomination for U.S. attorney general. According to Stephen Hess of the Washington-based Brookings Institution, although Baird's offence 'isn't like murder or arson and is something that is widely done and winked at, for the chief law enforcement officer it is not all right' (Corelli 1993, 42). Part of the hostility to Baird's candidacy stemmed from the frustration felt by ordinary Americans struggling to pay for legal child care (ibid).

6 Landed immigrants generally have access to the same citizenship rights as full citizens with the exception of voting in elections, running as political candidates, or taking up jobs involving national security. Landed immigrants are eligible to become citizens following three years of residence in Canada.

7 In 1990, the number of new entrants to the FDM program was 10,946, of which 60 per cent came from the Philippines. In 1991, 7,716 new domestic workers were accepted in Canada with 68 per cent coming from the Philippines (Mitchell 1993). Macklin (1992), who adds the number of domestics from the Philippines and the Caribbean to the number from the 'Other' category coming from Less Developed Countries, estimates that approximately 75 per cent of FDM entrants in 1990 were Third World women.

8 For an elaboration of these points, see Arat-Koc (1991) and Daenzer (1991, 5).

9 Thus, the reason for denying Caribbean domestics the option of applying for landed immigrant status from within Canada was clearly stated in 1976 by

the Director of Recruitment and Selection, Foreign Service Region: 'Permanent admission means job mobility. The recruitment of non immigrants
strongly impedes the turnover of domestics' (quoted in Daenzer 1991, 183).

10 One estimate places the number of illegal nannies in Toronto alone at between
25,000 to 30,000 as of January 1993. Immigration lawyer Mendel Green asserts
that the new regulations attached to the LCP instituted in April 1992 have
'created a total illegal undersociety of nannies. If you were to go into Rosedale
and Bayview and Forest Hill [three affluent Toronto neighbourhoods], 70 per
cent of the nannies who work there are illegal' (Mitchell 1993).

11 Bernard Valcourt, then minister of Employment and Immigration, depicted
the process of consultation as one involving, 'domestic worker advocacy
groups, other federal government departments, provincial government
officials, national and municipal day care associations, employer and
employment agency representatives, academics and other concerned
individuals ... In making the changes, we have aimed for a balance between
the needs of domestic workers and employers' (Valcourt 1992).

12 According to a survey of 592 domestic workers in Toronto, only one third
(35 per cent) of live-in domestics worked the regular work week (in Ontario)
of 44 hours; 40 per cent worked for 45 to 50 hours; 18 per cent worked for 50
to 60 hours, and 6 per cent worked more than 60 hours a week. Moreover, an
overwhelming 44 per cent of those performing overtime work stated that
they received no compensation whatsoever. Another 22 per cent of live-in
domestic workers who did overtime work reported receiving less than legal
rates of compensation, whereas only 34 per cent received the legal compensation of $7.50 per hour or extra time off (Arat-Koc and Villasin 1990, 6).

13 INTERCEDE is the acronym for the International Coalition to End Domestic
Exploitation. Other domestic worker advocacy groups that have formed
since the 1970s (including some that are now defunct) are in Ontario: Multicultural Homeworkers Association; Labour Rights for Domestic Servants; in
Quebec: L'Association pour la Défense des Droits du Personnel Domestique;
in British Columbia: the West Coast Domestic Workers' Association; the
Committee for the Advancement of Domestic Workers; the Committee for
Domestic Workers' and Caregivers, and the Labour Advocacy Group (Macklin 1992, 691–2, n.46; Epstein 1983).

14 When a domestic worker's employment is terminated, the Immigration
Department usually allows the worker two weeks to find a new job. In 1986,
it was estimated that the Canadian Consolidated Revenue Fund received
almost two million dollars a year in deductions from the employment of
foreign domestics (Estable 1986, 35).

15 Immigration lawyers interviewed for a news story on the 'nanny shortage'

have observed that there has been no drop in demand for domestic workers during the recession (Mitchell 1993).

16 Regardless of the issue of individual strategies to deal with a paucity of available childcare options, some feminist theorists have turned to a strategic orientation towards the hiring of private nannies and maids as a generalized solution to the childcare crisis. This perspective indicates the extent to which class divisions have permeated contemporary feminist approaches, widening the gap between the strategic interests of middle-class women and those of immigrant and working-class women (see Barrett and McIntosh 1982, 144–5; for a critique see German 1989, 77–9; and Arat-Koc 1989; 1990).

17 A 1988 household income and expenditures survey in the Philippines revealed that fully 15.5 per cent of families in the Philippines receive income from abroad contributing about 30 per cent of their total incomes (Abella 1992, 3). Macklin (1992, 695ff) cites a recent survey by the West Coast Domestic Workers Association which indicated that '70 per cent of respondents sent money home monthly.'

18 The number and conduct of domestic placement agencies, like any industry dominated by small businesses, is highly varied. Only Ontario, Quebec and British Columbia have licensing procedures for this industry (Bakan and Stasiulis 1995).

19 In interviews with domestic placement agencies in Toronto, the employing Canadian family was assumed to be white and of European origin (see Bakan and Stasiulis 1995).

20 As Macklin elaborates, a white employer of a women of colour worker 'can hardly claim that [her employee] is ideally suited to domestic work because she is a woman without impugning herself, but she can fall back on [women of colour] being "naturally" hard working, subservient, loyal tidy housekeepers and "good with children"' (1993, 754; see also Glenn 1992, 32).

21 Racial/gendered ideologies and citizenship status (and hoped-for status) are, however, as we have shown throughout this article, related. The perception that the 'opportunity' to work in Canada is a privilege for women of colour from Third World countries is widespread, but such a discourse is generally not applied to white women from Europe, particularly if their first language is English (Arat-Koc 1991, 14–18).

22 It is likely, however, that more women from Eastern Europe than Western Europe will attempt to enter the LCP for the purpose of gaining landed status in Canada, given the greater economic and political instability in Eastern Europe. The numbers and proportion of the total entrants into the LCP from countries such as the Czech Republic and Slovak Republic rose in the 1990s (Canada, Citizenship and Immigration 1996).

23 For instance, the new Immigration Act legislated by the Mulroney Conservatives in 1992 requires some new immigrants to sign a contract, as a condition of their visa, obliging them to live in a certain place and follow a certain occupation for an unspecified amount of time (see Dan Heap 1992). In addition, migrant labour schemes since 1945 have continued to racialize noncitizen workers from the Caribbean despite the liberalization of Canadian immigration law that occurred in the 1960s (Satzewich 1989; 1991).

24 A recent Supreme Court decision in the Philippines ruled that 'Filipinos who become citizens in other countries lose their right to own and acquire land in the Philippines' ('Ex-Pinoys Lose' 1992, 1–2).

25 The controversy around the appointment of prospective U.S. Attorney General Zoe Baird, referred to earlier, is a case in point. Some of the outrage came from American feminists, including leaders of the National Organization of Women, concerned that female government appointees were subject to scrutiny not normally applied to male candidates (*Globe and Mail*, 11 February 1993). Martin Loney aptly noted, however, that 'the well-heeled feminists, who have led the cries of outrage, have been markedly silent on the injustices of class and ethnicity revealed by this case ... Illegal immigrants in the U.S., whether in agriculture or domestic service, constitute an underclass, deprived of health care, pensions and other benefits ... Perhaps this case tells us as much about the mores of upper-income American women as about gender attitudes in that country' (Loney 1993).

2

From 'Mothers of the Nation' to Migrant Workers

SEDEF ARAT-KOC

In the last two decades, the legal status of foreign domestic workers in Canada has worsened. In all countries where there are paid domestic workers, gender and class inequalities have largely structured their socio-legal status and working conditions. In Canada, however, historical variations in the status and conditions of domestic workers have more directly been linked to the histories of racism and immigration. Precisely at a time in Canadian history when citizenship rights were generally improving for women, the status and conditions of foreign domestic workers in Canada significantly deteriorated. In line with other analyses (Bakan and Stasiulis, this volume; Daenzer 1993; Villasin and Phillips 1994), this chapter argues that changes in the racial/ethnic composition of migrant domestic workers have played an important part in this deterioration, and traces the historically differential treatment domestic workers from different race/ethnic backgrounds and different source regions have received from Canadian society and the state. It focuses in particular on the different state and societal interests, policies, and practices regulating British domestics and those foreign domestics deemed to be from 'less desirable' backgrounds. As Daenzer (this volume) provides an in-depth analysis of the policies governing migrant domestics from the 1970s to the 'reforms' of the Live-in Caregiver Program in 1992, this chapter addresses only the period prior to the 1970s.

Race, Citizenship, and Domestic Workers

Hidden in the household and considered 'women's work,' domestic service has never enjoyed a favourable status in industrial capitalist society. Paid domestic servants have fared even worse in that, as working-class women, they have rarely shared the status of their middle- or upper-class mistresses. Moreover, nannies, housekeepers, cooks, and other types of caregivers working in the private sphere of the domestic family/household have not been considered to be 'real' workers. Excluded from the organized labour movement, they have lacked the organizational opportunities, sense of solidarity, and protections and benefits the labour movement has provided (see Judy Fudge, this volume).

Subordination has thus been a universal condition of domestic workers in industrial capitalism. In spite of these common features, there have also been significant variations in the status and conditions of domestic workers based on their relationship to membership in the Canadian state (e.g., as citizens or non-citizens) and within the socially constructed 'imagined community' of the Canadian nation. In Canada, race and ethnicity have been pivotal elements in defining a collectivity's membership in Canadian society and the national community, as well as relationship to the state.

This chapter focuses on the differences in state and societal treatment of white British domestics, and domestic workers from other racial/ethnic backgrounds. Whereas white British women were recruited as domestics, they were also sought after for their future or potential roles as wives and mothers of the Canadian nation, and thus as nation-builders and civilizers. In contrast, domestic workers with 'less preferred' racial/ethnic backgrounds were viewed merely as cheap, temporary, and expendable labour. The variations in, regulation of, and experiences of, different groups of domestic workers thus suggest that there has been a continuum in status and socially constructed racial/ethnic desirability among foreign domestics, which corresponds to the racial/ethnic hierarchy constructed within Canadian immigration policy as a whole.

Where one falls along this continuum has largely determined the possibility and legal conditions of entry into Canada, as well as the work, living standards, and rights enjoyed within the country. As the source countries of immigrant domestic workers have moved farther away from Britain and Europe, state regulation of foreign domestics has increased and become more coercive, and the work/living conditions and access to rights have subsequently worsened. Nonetheless, as discussed in this chapter, domestic workers have a long history of resisting the harsh and restrictive conditions meted out by state authorities, employers, and various immigration gatekeepers, to contest coercive and exclusionary practices.

Historically, immigration policies in Canada have been determined by several, at times conflicting, objectives. These have included the development of a white British society in Canada, establishing settler colonies in certain regions of the country (with previously sparse European populations), and meeting the needs of the labour market. Although Britain has been the preferred source country for immigration, other sources have been considered when the supply of British immigrants has been insufficient (Knowles 1992). The introduction of a point system in the 1960s to determine and rank entry qualifications replaced explicitly racist selection criteria with a purportedly objective system emphasizing labour-market requirements. Nonetheless, many authors have argued that racism continues to prevail in immigration policies and procedures (Arat-Koc 1992; Bolaria and Li 1988; Cohen 1994; Daenzer 1993; Law Union of Canada 1981; Satzewich 1989; Villasin and Phillips 1994).

British domestic workers coming to Canada at the turn of the century were regarded as 'daughters of the Empire' and 'mothers of the race.' While their status as members of the nation did not necessarily affect their conditions in domestic work, it did determine their access to employment and survival avenues outside domestic work. Even when British domestics were unable to improve their conditions at work, they could 'vote with their feet,' as it were, and leave domestic service for another employer, another job, or marriage. The options were far more restricted for domestics from the 'least desirable' racial/ethnic backgrounds, such as black domestic workers. As the latter were expected to aid in the reproduction of white families, the needs of their own families (often residing in other, underdeveloped countries) were officially and wilfully ignored. For women of colour, societal racism and direct state intervention in the form of immigration policies and regulations have delimited labour-market choices and undermined working conditions.

The history of foreign domestic workers in Canada suggests that there is a specific relationship between the rights enjoyed by domestics and their relationship to, or membership in, the Canadian nation and the state. Most modern states are characterized by hierarchies of citizenship rights. Contrary to a model of universal citizenship whereby citizenship rights are accessible to all members of a society, some groups lack many or most such rights (e.g., migrant labourers, slaves, or populations under occupation). Such groups can be said to exist within the boundaries of state regulation, but outside the boundaries of the national collectivity, and with lesser access to state-provided, citizenship (civil, political, and social) rights.

Women of colour, who have made up the majority of immigrant domestic workers arriving in Canada in the postwar period, are considered to be neither members of the Canadian nation nor citizen-members of the state. Even though, as non-citizens, women of colour arriving in the postwar period have lacked basic civil, political, and social rights, highly regulatory immigration practices have ensured that they are very much inside the state.[1] This has meant that while their conditions of work have been under-regulated, domestic workers themselves, especially those from the 'least desirable' backgrounds, have become over-regulated.

The remainder of this chapter explores and accounts for the historically divergent forms of state regulation and conditions of white and non-white domestic workers in Canada, from Britain, other European, and Third World countries such as Jamaica. No group of domestic workers in Canada who have entered the ambiguous and fraught social space of the private family/household has been exempt from exploitation, close supervision, and restricted rights and employment standards (in comparison with most other groups of workers in 'public' workplaces). Nonetheless, the manner in which race/ethnicity, gender, and class have combined have more severely circumscribed the rights and opportunities for non-British women, and especially women of colour, in comparison with white, British women.

Racism, Immigration, and Domestic Service

In Europe, class and gender inequalities were the main determinants of relationships in domestic service. In Canada, as well as in other settler colonies such as Australia and New Zealand, racial and ethnic inequalities also played a very important part (Stasiulis and Jhappan 1995). Immigration policies and practices have been key mechanisms in regulating the racial/ethnic composition of immigrant domestic workers and determining the status, conditions, and autonomy of those who have been allowed in. Through immigration policy, membership in the Canadian nation and state, and access to citizenship rights, have been regulated. Access to citizenship rights has been facilitated for domestics of the 'desirable' race/ethnicity, while made difficult or inaccessible for those of 'undesirable' racial/ethnic backgrounds.

In Canada, domestic service has historically been associated with forms of 'unfree labour,' including indenture, and less commonly, slavery (see Miles 1987). Domestic servants from abroad were rarely recruited as free wage labourers, with the same access to choice of employers, occupations, or workplaces that this class of workers nominally enjoyed. While much smaller in scale than the slavery characterizing the plantation system of the southern United States, slavery did exist in Canada until its gradual elimination in the late eighteenth and early nineteenth centuries. The first Canadian slaves were Native peoples, frequently Pawnee (or Panis, as they came to be called in New France). Black slaves were also brought north from the United States by their employers, who were often United Empire Loyalists. The vast majority of female slaves were employed as domestic servants (Barber 1991, 3; Bolaria and Li 1988, 165). Pervasive anti-black racism continued even once slavery was abolished in Canada, and meant that black women had few labour market options beyond domestic service. As late as the 1940s, Brand estimates that at least 80 per cent of black women in Canadian cities worked in domestic service (Brand 1991).

At different times, some groups of white immigrant women who were recruited to provide domestic service also entered as unfree labour (e.g., on a one-year indenture program). This entry status did not have the same consequences for their future status and conditions in Canada, however. For many white women, domestic service was only a stage of life, and a bridge to a different life. In New France, domestic service was often performed by *engagés*, indentured servants from France whose passage had been paid in advance by their future employers. Given concerns with the small population of the white colony and the even smaller numbers of women, *engagés* were encouraged to marry immediately after the end of their bond. In some cases, they were even allowed to break their contract on condition of marriage (Barber 1991, 3; Prentice et al. 1988, 46).

In the early nineteenth century, in the rural areas of Canada and the northern United States, local white women who were hired as domestics experienced less rigid status differences in relation to their employers. Called 'help' instead of 'servants,' these were women who were hired for short periods of time to contribute to their families' income and to aid neighbours in coping with the demands of illness, harvest season, or the care of numerous children. Employed by farmers and small shopkeepers, these workers cooperated with employers in the hard work of the family economy. The exploitative relationship of 'help' to their employers was moderated insofar as they shared the conditions and the tables of the families for whom they worked. They often 'demanded treatment in accord with their status as a member of another family of "independent worth"' (Barber 1991, 4). Distinguishing 'help' from past and future groups of domestic workers was the fact that theirs was less an occupation than an activity that allowed casual, temporary, and/or part-time employment (Dudden 1983, 12–43).

The conditions of domestic workers in the rural areas contrasted sharply, however, with relations in propertied households of the cities where the social distance between employers and employees was growing. So significant were the rural/urban differences that *The Canadian Settlers' Handbook* advised prospective immigrant domestics that they would enjoy 'social amenities' in rural Canada, but that 'no lady should dream of going as a home-help in the cities, for there class distinctions (were) as rampant as in England' (cited in Lenskyj 1981, 10).

From the mid-nineteenth century to the 1920s, changes in domestic service that had occurred earlier in Europe as a result of the development of capitalism, industrialization, and urbanization also prevailed in North America. As the urban middle-class family became more privatized, its emphasis on domestic comforts and luxury increased, thus contributing to an increase in the demand for domestic workers. Changes in the nature of work, and among the workers performing this type of work, precluded improvements in working and living conditions for domestic workers. The separation of the public and private sphere and the decline in the general status of the domestic sphere coincided with the rapid development of domestic service as a women's job ghetto. Between the early and late nineteenth century, within a period of approximately sixty years, the percentage of women among urban domestic workers grew from 50 per cent to 90 per cent (Lacelle 1987).

Further contributing to a decline in the status of servants, or alternatively, in certain regions, the persistence of their low status, was the availability of groups of vulnerable workers. In the United States, for example, in regions where there were large concentrations of people of colour and where racism was prevalent, it was usually women of the oppressed racial/ethnic groups who had no choice but to accept domestic service positions. Despite differences in the composition of populations and the mix of industries in the regions, there were important similarities in the situation of Mexicans in the Southwest, African Americans in the South, and Japanese people in northern California and Hawaii. Each of these groups was placed in a separate legal category from whites, and excluded from rights and protections accorded to full citizens (Glenn 1992, 8).

In Canada and the northeastern United States, different groups of white immigrants, who were perceived as socially and indeed 'racially' inferior to the ethnically dominant white population, also provided a source of vulnerable labour during certain historical periods. In the 1870s, Irish women, who had fled economic desperation at home, found almost no alternatives to domestic work in Canada. In all Canadian urban centres except Quebec City, female Irish immigrants were so highly represented among domestics that domestic service came to be identified with Irish women (Lacelle 1987). The term 'servant,' rarely used earlier in the nineteenth century to refer to white domestics, was reintroduced as immigrants replaced Canadian-born whites as the dominant group of domestic workers (Rollins 1985, 51–2). Lacelle (1987) found that over the course of the nineteenth century, popular perceptions of domestics became more unfavourable, the level of discipline to which domestic workers were subject increased, and their working conditions deteriorated.

It was in the late nineteenth century that immigration began to be used systematically to recruit and control domestic workers. This was a time when the demand for domestic workers increased while the supply among Canadian-born women declined. The growth in demand corresponded to the high standards of housekeeping of a rising urban middle class at a time when household technology remained underdeveloped and housework extremely laborious. The decline in supply of workers willing and available to undertake domestic service was accounted for by industrialization, which opened up new labour market options for working-class women – in factories, hospitals, offices, retail outlets, and schools. The conditions of domestic work, especially live-in service, were so unfavourable that Canadian-born working-class women refused to accept it, even when the pay in other employment was lower. As Canadian-born women came to shun the isolating and menial conditions of domestic service, ever-greater efforts were made to recruit immigrant women to meet the unabating demand.

The solution sought to this shortage both by the state and a vibrant middle-class social reform movement 'focused more on maintaining the supply of workers through carefully supervised immigration than on reforming the conditions of household work' (Barber 1987, 100). White British middle- and upper-class women, active in social reform, were more interested in the protection of the private virtue of single, young

British 'girls,' who were to be the future 'mothers of the nation,' than in alleviating the exploitation of domestic labourers. In the early twentieth century, more than one third of domestic workers in Canada were foreign-born (Barber 1991, 7–8). In some regions, such as western Canada, the proportion was much higher. In 1891, in Winnipeg, for instance, as many as 84 per cent of domestic workers were born outside of Canada (Barber 1987, 100).

While the demands of the labour market for domestic workers encouraged recruitment of workers from abroad, the dominant forces in Canadian society and the state were selective regarding the source countries for recruitment. In the period following Confederation, the state began not only to regulate immigration through legislation, but also to use immigration policy as the major means of actively controlling the racial composition of Canada. While recruitment of non-white immigrants for special labour-intensive projects did occur in the post-Confederation period, racist immigration legislation and regulations were enacted to quell non-white immigration. Immediately after the completion of the transcontinental railway in 1885, for example, which relied on the back-breaking labour of some 15,000 Chinese workers, the government passed a Chinese Immigration Act that imposed steep head taxes on Chinese immigrants (Law Union of Canada 1981, 20–2). Unique sets of regulations, which clearly sought to rationalize and mystify the denial of the rights of 'British subjects' in the Dominion of Canada, also severely restricted the entry of South Asians, Japanese, black Americans, and West Indians, as well as access of these non-white groups to state entitlements and citizenship rights, or symbolically recognized membership in the Canadian nation.

In the early twentieth century, British women constituted more than three-quarters of immigrant domestics coming to Canada. A number of immigration schemes were introduced in the late nineteenth and early twentieth centuries specifically aimed at attracting white British women to Canada. The treatment of British domestics under these schemes reflects a complex intersection of biases and contradictions based on gender, class, race, and nationality. While the amount of planning and energy involved in immigration schemes tell us a great deal about how desirable these women were as immigrants in terms of their racial/ethnic stock and the demand for their intended occupation, their working conditions as well as the paternalistic treatment they endured reflect a subordinate class and gender status.

British Domestic Schemes and Nation-Building in Canada

To make sense of Canada's approach to British domestic workers in the late nineteenth and early twentieth centuries, we need to place it in the context of racialized/gender roles within discourses of nation-building. White, and especially white British, women were a powerful symbol in the transition of Canada from fur-trade to settler society, most apparent in the Canadian prairies. Prior to their arrival, white trader men had commonly entered into marriage with Native and 'mixed-breed' women (van Kirk 1983), a practice that ended abruptly with the entry of white women. As dependence on Native people to sustain the economy weakened, direct and forceful attempts at assimilation became the most typical ways white settler society dealt with Native cultures and peoples, with devastating consequences for the latter.

The arrival of white women in western Canada underlined the permanence of settlement and the conscious effort to define Canada as a British society. In their roles as mothers and culture-bearers, white British women were expected to help entrench British culture in Canada and pass it on to future generations. Through their ethical role as 'God's police,' they were also expected to contribute to the creation of a more 'stable' and 'respectable' colonial society (Buckley 1977, 26).

The importance of British women in the colonies was stressed in imperial designs on both sides of the Atlantic. In Britain, female emigration was emphasized by some as perhaps the most important part of empire-building: 'As respects morals and manners, it is of little importance what colonial fathers are in comparison to colonial mothers' (cited in Roberts 1976, 108). The absence of the civilizing influence of white women, it was maintained, could result in irresponsibility and immorality in a colony of all white males. Men, in this view, 'never bec[a]me anchored until they marr[ied]' the right type of women (cited in Roberts 1979, 191). In a colony with a balanced sex ratio between male and female colonizers, on the other hand, 'every pair of immigrants would have the strongest motives for industry, shrewdness, and thrift' (cited in Roberts 1976, 108).

In the racist discourse of nation-building, class biases also shaped the perceived appropriateness of women as settlers. While women of the 'right' racial/ethnic stock were thought to be culture-bearers and civilizers, 'civilization' was not thought of as a universal attribute of all women. Helen Reid, a social worker in Montreal, resorted to eugenics in asserting that working-class women were not fit to settle in Canada. In her view, working-class women would

> in addition to their lack of training for domestic service, bring with them only too often, serious mental and moral disabilities. These women either glut the labour market here, reducing the wages of working men, or end up alas! too frequently in our jails, hospitals or asylums. (Cited in Valverde 1991, 126)

Only women from a certain class background and of 'virtuous' character could embody and transmit the ideals of civilization, as defined by British and British-Canadian authorities and moral reform leaders. The 'elevation of morals' in the colonies could only be the 'result of the mere presence in the colony of a number of high class women.' It was important, therefore, to maintain 'an influx into the colonies of a body of women infinitely superior by birth, by education, and by taste, to the hordes of wild uneducated creatures ... hitherto sent abroad' (cited in Roberts 1976, 110).

There was a contradiction between the economic dimension of colonization and its ideological dimension as a 'civilizing' force. The labour requirements of the colonies demanded the strenuous labour of women on farms and in domestic work. Women of middle and upper classes, however, who were thought to be the ideal colonizers and civilizers, could hardly be ideal candidates for the drudgery of domestic service or the challenges of pioneer farming.

The tension between the conflicting demands of colonization was partially solved in the nineteenth century with the availability in Britain of a huge 'surplus' of 'distressed' gentlewomen. These were single women from middle-class and educated backgrounds, who were impoverished by economic circumstances or the death of a spouse. At a time in Britain when an unfavourable male/female ratio limited women's marriage prospects and when white-collar jobs were not open to women, the options for destitute gentlewomen were restricted. Given their middle-class identity and norms of respectability, these women considered working-class jobs unsuitable avenues of employment. It was only by leaving Britain that they could find a means of survival, while maintaining respectability (Jackel 1982, xxi).

The plight of impoverished British gentlewomen in the nineteenth century was of concern to reformers and philanthropists in both Britain and in the colonies (Buckley 1977; Jackel 1982; Roberts 1976; 1979; 1990).

The interest in alleviating the desperation of gentlewomen 'at home' in Britain neatly coincided with the nation-building vision of British and Canadian elites. For the latter, 'the nation' that Canada was in the process of building, 'was not solely an economic entity, not ... merely a matter of railroads, national markets and entrepreneurship ... It was rather the embodiment of a certain spirit in a developing human community' (Roberts 1979, 186). The cornerstone of the nation was the family and the cornerstone of the family was women. The best way to build a nation of white settlers, therefore, was to help bring the 'best classes' of British women to Canada.

> It would be impossible to speak too strongly about the need of a wife and mother for the settler's home. As a sympathetic companion, an economical manager, an actual helpmeet in the farm work, as a mother of future citizens, and as a standard bearer of civilization, she will always be invaluable. (Cited in Roberts 1979, 187)

As to the appropriateness of employing the 'best classes' of British women in what was considered to be 'menial' work, some simply took a matter-of-fact attitude on the question stating that 'every woman is a servant where labour is so scarce' (cited in Jackel 1982, xviii).

The late nineteenth century was still a period when immigration was not totally formalized and bureaucratized by the state. As part of the reform movement, many middle-class women took an active part in female immigration work through women's organizations. These women were also usually the employers of domestic workers. Active in social reform, charitable, or sometimes feminist organizations, middle-class women in late nineteenth century Canadian society 'were urged to delegate the household tasks which had previously occupied most of their time, in order that their civilizing influence no longer be confined to home and family' (Lenskyj 1981, 4).

Immigration work by female reformers was directed at recruitment of domestic workers, their 'protection' during transportation, and their placement upon arrival. While class interests and labour force demand for domestic workers were important motivations leading women reformers to become involved in immigration matters, their interests in immigration needs to be distinguished from those of business, transportation agents, and state authorities. Aware that British female immigrants would become the 'daughters of the Empire' and 'mothers of the race,' female reformers were as much concerned about the 'quality' of recruits as their numbers and the potential economic benefits they would bring to Canada (Roberts 1979, 1990). Caroline Chisholm, who was involved in emigration work on the other side of the Atlantic, also expressed this point of view: 'I should not feel the interest I do in female emigration, if I did not look beyond providing families with female servants. If I did not know how much they are required as wives, and how much moral good they may spread forth in society as wives' (cited in Roberts 1976, 119).

The incessant concern shown for the 'quality' of female immigrants was not always experienced as a privilege by immigrant domestics even if they were of the 'right stock' and of a respectable class background. For women, true 'belonging' in the nation was conditional upon living up to the idealized standards of Victorian morality. Poor, single women, even those from a 'gentle' background, could not be trusted to maintain high moral standards, particularly in view of the untamed moral character of men and the temptations associated with 'white slavery,' such as a love for finery (Valverde 1991). Therefore, middle-class women who were involved with emigration and immigration societies in Britain and Canada did not hesitate to recruit selectively and to closely monitor and curtail the freedoms of the chosen ones. British emigration societies, in collaboration with Canadian organizations like the National Council of Women of Canada, required very strict recruitment and screening procedures. In addition to references and a personal interview, they were responsible for introducing a compulsory medical examination, which was later extended to all immigrants (Lenskyj 1981, 8; Valverde 1991, 126).

Horrified by conditions on steamships crossing the Atlantic, women's organizations also took on the responsibility to 'protect' and supervise women during their overseas voyage. Immigrant women usually travelled under the supervision of matrons, who were women of middle- or upper-class backgrounds. 'The idle and frivolous habits encouraged and or contracted on board ship' could make women unfit for their duties in the colony; thus, it was imperative to keep 'strict discipline and industrious habits among emigrants, especially among women' (cited in Roberts 1976, 111). Matrons supervising parties of women carefully watched their charges to make sure they would not waste their time or befriend unsuitable acquaintances. Once they arrived in Canada, women were taken into hostels and shelters supervised by women's groups, and then accompanied to their final destination (Roberts 1979). The sense of curtailment of freedom is aptly captured in the following account by one migrant British domestic:

We all wondered if we were coming to a civilized country, for we were brought from the ship as though we were prisoners, and had to sit in a room, and hardly dared move, let alone speak. We were not allowed to bid goodbye to our friends we had made during the voyage, and in fact I think they thought we were heathens. Several passengers passed the remark as we were driven as cattle. (Cited in Lenskyj 1981, 9)

While claiming that their philanthropic immigration work was for the 'protection' of immigrant women, and especially of their continuously imperiled respectability, these middle-class women's reform groups did not hesitate to cooperate with authorities in the deportation of 'unsuitable' immigrants. In what Valverde calls 'philanthropic deportation,' women immigrationists participated in the deportation of significant numbers of domestic workers (Valverde 1991, 124–7).[2]

The treatment of British domestic workers in Canada at the turn of the century thus demonstrates the complexity of relations among gender, class, nationality, and race. Compared to domestics from other racial/ ethnic backgrounds who came before and after them, British domestics enjoyed a very privileged position. Unlike domestics from other backgrounds, they were unquestionably accepted as legitimate members of the Canadian society and nation. If they lived up to 'appropriate' Victorian standards of 'true womanhood,' they were also regarded as civilizers and nation-builders. Unlike other groups, British domestics at the turn of the century were brought to Canada for more than their capacity to labour as domestic workers. Seen as potential 'mothers of the nation,' British domestics rarely stayed in domestic work for long periods of time. Viewed as 'desirable' immigrants by state authorities and reform movements alike, British domestics also were able to benefit from assisted passage in their arrival to Canada.[3]

The sense that white British domestic workers were 'privileged,' must, however, be moderated by the knowledge of their subjection to extensive social control. Even though their racial/ethnic composition made British domestics a desirable group of immigrants, neither the demand for their work nor the desirability of their background guaranteed better working conditions. The ways in which British domestics were 'protected' and 'helped' by women reformers not only limited the freedom of domestics as women and as persons, but generally reflected the class differences between the two groups. The subordination of British domestics placed the needs of women immigrationists as employers above those of domestics as workers. Segregated during the voyage, and upon reception, isolated in boarding-houses and in their employers' households, the opportunities for domestics to associate with other immigrants and workers, and to learn about alternative job opportunities, were highly restricted. The conditions in domestic work remained so unfavourable that indenture often became the only insurance that domestics would stay with their assigned employer.

Between 1888 and the 1920s, when the government did not directly provide assisted passage, private agents arranged for advanced loans from employers, which would tie domestics to them for a specific length of time. The Department of Immigration sometimes ignored protective legislation in order to fulfil its policing function. Around the turn of the century, for example, master and servant legislation was passed in most of the provinces, to protect domestics from exploitative contracts that they might have signed in order to immigrate to Canada. According to this legislation, contracts signed outside the province were not legally binding. The Immigration Department, however, circumvented this legislation by having domestics resign their contract upon arrival in Canada, thus enforcing their indentured status (Leslie 1974, 122).

Being of the desirable racial/ethnic stock was also not necessarily experienced as a privilege by the 80,000 British children who were brought in as indentured farm and domestic help to Canadian farms. Between 1868 and 1925, concerns with imperial nation-building and the health of the British race led to efforts by emigrationists to remove working-class children from urban slums and rescue-homes in Britain and place them in what was considered to be the beneficial environment and 'healthy family life' of colonial farms. In a period when changing conceptions of childhood and approaches to child labour were already favourably affecting working-class children in Britain, these children were not only exploited as workers, but sometimes shunned for potential criminal tendencies and moral and physical degeneracies (Parr 1980).

Non-British, European Domestic Workers

As the Canadian state failed to fulfil its objectives to populate western Canada and meet Canada's labour needs through an exclusively British source of immigration, other sources of immigrants were sought. In the late nineteenth century, continental Europe and the United States were considered the least objectionable alternative sources to Britain. Women from Scandinavian countries and Central and Eastern Europe came to Canada as daughters of agricultural families settling in the prairies, or as single workers. There was a substantial increase in the number of non-British domestics in the 1920s. By the early 1930s, as many as one-quarter of immigrant domestic workers coming to Ontario were from these regions of continental Europe (Prentice et al. 1988, 222). In the mid-twentieth century, other sources, such as Southern Europe, were also considered.

Scandinavian Domestic Workers

In the early twentieth century, Scandinavian countries were a favoured source of domestic workers, second only to Britain. Among Scandinavians, Finnish women predominated in domestic service. Even in the midst of the Depression, in 1937, Canada started a special scheme to bring in domestics from this region. To encourage immigration of Finnish and other Scandinavian domestics, the Canadian government 'bent immigration regulations, created special categories and made easier travel arrangements' (Lindstrom-Best 1986b, 34, 36).

An overwhelming majority of Finnish women who came to Canada in the early twentieth century were occupied in domestic service. In Winnipeg, for example, with the exception of a few who worked in restaurants, almost all Finnish women were domestic workers. When Canadian-born women and British immigrants were starting to move to other jobs in the labour market, Finnish women remained concentrated in domestic work. Despite the diversity of skills they brought to Canada, the employment options of Finnish women were limited by their lack of fluency in the English language (Lindstrom-Best 1986b, 35).

Lindstrom-Best argues that Finnish domestic workers were 'proud maids' who enjoyed a high status in the Finnish community and relatively favourable conditions at work. Because most women in the Finnish community in Canada were domestic workers, class divisions were absent among women of the same ethnocultural background. Thus, class, gender, and ethnocultural solidarity facilitated the emergence of a proud collective image and organizations dedicated to improving working opportunities and conditions. Also contributing to their collective strength was the labour and socialist organizing traditions many Finnish immigrants brought with them to Canada. Some ethnic organizations served as virtual labour locals. In addition, the Finns built 'immigrant homes' in several cities and started employment services for domestic workers. In this climate of class, gender, and ethnic solidarity, Finnish domestics were able to share information, and refuse low wages and bad working conditions. Even in their first year in Canada, many were able to change jobs frequently in order to ensure improved conditions and resist the slave-like treatment normally accorded to recent immigrant domestics (Lindstrom-Best 1986a; 1986b).

Central and Eastern European Domestics

The majority of Central and Eastern European domestics went to western Canada. The number of immigrants from the British Isles was insufficient to fulfil the defined objectives of populating western Canada – securing that territory against the United States, and developing an agrarian-based economy. The pressure to admit 'non-preferred' Central and Eastern European immigrants also came from the railway companies, which wanted to increase their business in western Canada. In 1925, the federal government signed a Railways Agreement with the Canadian Pacific Railway and the Canadian National Railway that authorized the two companies to recruit and place farmers and domestics (Barber 1987, 108). In the years following the Railways Agreement, the number of domestic workers coming to western Canada from continental Europe grew significantly. In Manitoba, in 1921, the British made up 60 per cent of immigrant domestics, while continental Europeans comprised 30 per cent. By 1931, the ratios were almost reversed (Barber 1987, 109). Unlike the preferred British domestics, domestic workers coming from continental Europe were not given assisted passage (Barber 1991, 16). Most domestics from Central and Eastern Europe were considered to be 'of the peasant type'; their assumed unfamiliarity with standards and equipment of housework in middle-class homes deemed them suitable only for rural households.

Among Central and Eastern Europeans, however, there was one group of domestics who were preferred for urban employment. These were the daughters of Russian Mennonites who came to Canada as refugees, and were themselves from servant-employing backgrounds. While women reformers had concentrated most of their energy and attention on British domestics, most of the Central and Eastern European immigration took place outside their control. The Mennonites were able to establish *Maedchenheim*, or Girls' Homes, in several cities, including Vancouver, Saskatoon, Regina, Winnipeg, and Toronto. Similar to Canadian Women's Hostels for British domestics, which were run by women reformers, the *Maedchenheim* offered temporary shelters for new arrivals and served as social centres. Unlike the Canadian Women's Hostels, however, but in common with the Finnish Immigrant Homes, these centres had no connections to employers; therefore, they worked to protect domestic workers. They would accompany the domestic to her place of employment, inspect the house with her, remove domestics from unfavourable working environments, and keep a blacklist of employers to whom they would refuse to send domestic workers (Barber 1987; 1991, 16–18).

During and following the Great Depression, when many Canadian-born women lost the few alternative sources of employment open to them, domestic work became once again the major employer of women as a whole. Despite the dire state of the economy, there was actually an increase during the 'dirty thirties' in the numbers of domestic workers. A generalized fall in wages and prices meant that families with fixed or steady incomes, who previously could not afford domestic workers, now had the means to do so (Prentice et al. 1988, 235–6). During this period, married women joined single women in returning to domestic work on a live-out, or sometimes live-in basis, while their unemployed husbands stayed home with the children (Barber 1991, 18). Central and Eastern European domestics who had come to Canada in the late 1920s faced special difficulties. They could only find work characterized by exceptionally low wages and dreadful working conditions (Barber 1991, 19).

Following the trend in Canadian history begun in the nineteenth century, the demand for domestic workers in the post–World War Two period again exceeded the supply. And once again, the Canadian state was involved in recruiting from foreign sources, with vulnerable groups providing the obvious recruits. Racism would play an important role in determining which of several vulnerable groups would be recruited. In the postwar period, the first group of immigrant domestic workers selected were refugee women in the displaced persons (DP) camps in Europe. Between 1947 and 1952, Canada accepted some 165,000 displaced persons on the condition that they would work under a one-year contract in specific occupations, where the wages and working conditions were unacceptable for Canadians. Men were to be accepted as agricultural workers, miners, and loggers; women were to be allowed in as domestic workers in institutions, such as hospitals, sanatoria, orphanages, and mental institutions, as well as private homes (Barber 1991, 19; Danys 1986, 76–7).

Humanitarian considerations took a back seat to economic motivations and ethnic considerations in the selection and immigration of DPs. The Canadian state not only specified the occupations in which refugees would work, but also indicated ethnic and religious preferences. Even though the Department of Immigration never produced statistics to show ethnic and religious distribution, racist considerations are very apparent in Department memos. For domestic workers, there was a clear preference for those coming from the Baltic countries of Estonia, Latvia, and Lithuania. It was thought that these women would be closest to the Scandinavians who were the preferred domestics among continental Europeans. There was also a preference for Protestants, even though they were a minority among DPs. Jewish women were considered to be unsuitable, ostensibly because very few Jews had had previous experience in domestic service. The government did experiment, however, with a few Jewish domestics in Jewish homes (Barber 1991, 19–20; Danys 1986, 130).

The recruitment criteria reflected common gender and class assumptions long applied to domestic workers. They seemed, however, to be more severe than in previous periods, given the conditions of refugees in postwar Europe. To qualify under the program, women had to be single or widowed, between eighteen and forty years of age, and of 'good average intelligence and emotional stability.' They were compelled to go through strict medical examinations, which included x-rays and tests for pregnancy and venereal diseases (Danys 1986, 133). Those who qualified signed a contract to remain in domestic service for one year. Even though prospective employers also filled out a form specifying wages and conditions of work, there was no regulation compelling employers even to show the form to their domestic employees (Danys 1986, 133).

Daenzer argues that the case of DP domestics constitutes a turning point in the nature and meaning of indenture for immigrant domestic workers. In this period, the agreement to stay in domestic service for one year changed from a friendly 'gentleperson's agreement' to a mandatory imposition (Daenzer 1993, 19). There were, however, no serious sanctions as yet for the non-fulfilment of contract. Another difference from the immigrant domestic schemes to follow was the ease with which domestics could change employers. Arthur MacNamara, the deputy minister of Labour who designed the DP program, made it a policy that any DP who asked for a transfer was to be given one (Danys 1986, 157). Despite the relative flexibility of the program, though, most DP domestics fulfilled their contract. Usually they remained with the same employer, motivated in part by gratitude to the Canadian government for the chance of a new life distant from their war-torn (and often Soviet-occupied) countries, as well as by fear of jeopardizing the chances for emigration of DPs still in camps (Barber 1991, 20).

Southern European Domestic Workers

Young single women in the DP camps were relatively scarce; moreover, Canada was forced to compete for potential domestic recruits with other countries in need of domestic workers. As a result, refugee domestics became only a temporary solution to the problem of domestic labour shortage. In the early 1950s, Canada once again introduced a policy of assisted passage. The government made several attempts, though not entirely successful, to recruit from the preferred source regions of Great Britain and Western Europe. With the exceptions of Germany and Holland, these attempts remained futile. With the entrenchment of the Cold War came the end of any possibility of emigration from Eastern Europe. Only then did Canada decide to experiment with domestic schemes drawing from countries in the least-preferred part of Europe: Southern Europe (Barber 1991, 21–3).

The approach of the Canadian state to Italian immigration in the 1950s demonstrates how the conflicting immigration priorities of meeting labour-market requirements and populating Canada with people of preferred races were played out. In the dominant racist view, while northern Italians were closer in temperament and moral fibre to other (relatively acceptable) Northern Europeans, Italians from the rural areas in southern Italy were equated with hot climate, hot temperaments, dark skins, cultural backwardness, and undemocratic traditions 'better suited to the "fragile" politics of Latin America' (Iacovetta 1992, 22). Despite this perception, however, pressures from business in the booming economy of the postwar period compelled the government to decide that the presence of southern Italians could be tolerated provided they offered hard work and cheap labour in agriculture, mining, railway repair, and construction (Iacovetta 1986, 14).

A domestic scheme was also started in 1951, but ended the following year after only 357 Italian women were recruited. The Italian domestic scheme was similar to the one that brought in refugee women from DP camps. Prospective employers in Canada would submit 'orders' for domestic workers and interested workers in Italy would sign a contract obliging them to stay in the designated occupation with the assigned employer for one year (Iacovetta 1986, 14; 1992, 34–6). Even though Canada had reintroduced the Assisted Passage Loan Scheme for domestics from Western Europe and Britain, it refused initially to extend it to Italian domestics and tried to persuade the Italian government, instead, to advance the passage fares (Iacovetta 1986, 15–16).

The short life of the program was attributable to the negative evaluation of domestics by the employers and by the state, as well as a decided lack of enthusiasm for the scheme on the part of Italian women. Italian domestics were seen as ignorant, 'primitive villagers' whose backward cultural background had failed to prepare them for the high standards and sophisticated technology of Canadian housekeeping. They were also found to be feisty employees who complained about working conditions, demanded to change employers, or simply left domestic work before the end of their contracts to work in the factories and/or join family members in Canada (Iacovetta 1986; 1992). Such demonstrations of freedom were not to be tolerated among an immigrant group of women who were not desired as 'mothers of the race' or carriers of culture. Italian domestics, like other non-British domestics, were brought into Canada solely for the cheap labour they were expected to provide in jobs that Canadians spurned.

There were two other Southern European countries – Greece and Spain – which Canada involved in domestic schemes during the early postwar years. In a period of otherwise restricted immigration from Greece, domestic workers started to be admitted in 1956 to be placed with Greek employers. This program, which brought in approximately 300 Greek women per year, lasted until 1966. A much more limited experiment, involving only 50 Spanish women, took place in 1959–60. Placement difficulties brought an end to this program when Spanish authorities desired Catholic homes, but most prospective employers were Protestant (Barber 1991, 22–3).

Women of Colour in Domestic Work

Domestic workers from different regions of Europe experienced different levels of vulnerability in their relations with the Canadian state and society, depending on British-Canadian stereotypes, political circumstances at the time of immigration to Canada, and their own traditions and prospects for resistance. Thus, while all foreign domestics have experienced varying degrees of coercion by the state and more powerful groups, European domestics have fallen along different points in the continuum of the treatment of immigrant domestic workers in Canada. Compared to British domestics, non-white domestic workers stand at the opposite end of this continuum. While women of colour in Canada have commonly been ghettoized into domestic labour, as migrant domestics, they were only permitted by state authorities to enter Canada as a last resort if recruitment from British and other European sources failed. Since the 1960s, the 'liberalized' immigration policies have not expressed any explicit bias against domestics from non-European sources. Indeed, women from the Third World have predominated among immigrant domestic workers since the early 1970s. The current social and political acceptability, however, of a status and conditions for domestic workers that would have been unacceptable half a century ago, suggest that racialized sexism and gendered racism are alive and well in Canadian society and immigration policy.

Beginning with black slaves who provided domestic service for nuns and other employers in New France, women of colour in Canada have been a source of domestic workers during most of Canadian history, largely because they have been barred from exercising other labour-market options. Long after the abolition of slavery at the end of the eighteenth century, black women in Canada remained in domestic work. They did find industrial employment at a time of labour shortage during World War Two, but were subsequently the first group to be laid off (Brand 1991). At the turn of the century, Micmac women in Nova Scotia were also excluded from industrial employment and considered suited only for domestic work (Prentice et al. 1988, 121). In the postwar period, when Canada was considering immigration of domestics from among European refugees, Canadian employers also utilized the cheap labour of 'Canada's own displaced persons,' the Japanese Canadians (Light and Pierson 1990, 258).

Even though employers demonstrated that they would accept domestic labour from any background, providing the workers were cheap and docile, racial/ethnic considerations, which have long been a priority among top immigration authorities, often dictated against an open-door policy in immigration. As long as recruits could be found from 'preferred' or at least 'unobjectionable' sources, Canada avoided non-white immigrants. A clause in the Immigration Act of 1910, which was not removed until 1967, gave the government of Canada the legal power to discriminate on the basis of race (Satzewich 1989). This clause stated that the government could prohibit entry of immigrants belonging to 'any race deemed unsuited to the climate or requirements of Canada' (quoted in Calliste 1993/4, 133).

In 1911, there was a short-lived experiment with domestic workers from the Caribbean. With permission from the government, employers in Quebec arranged the immigration of approximately 100 French-speaking domestics from Guadeloupe. Racist assumptions about black women's sexuality played an important part in the perception of these domestics by the public. The press also fabricated stories and fuelled fears of immorality. Even though the employers, in their own paternalistic manner, generally responded positively to the women, preferring them to 'fussy' Canadian domestics, the government rejected the next round of applicants from Guadeloupe on the grounds of physical and moral unsuitability (Calliste 1989; Mackenzie 1988).

During the recession of 1913–15, when unemployed Canadians were willing to take any work, including domestic work, the government deported many Caribbean domestics already in Canada on the grounds that they could become 'public charges.' More important than economic considerations in this deportation was the fact that black domestic workers were, unlike their British counterparts, accepted only for their labour power, not as 'permanent assets' capable of contributing to the social and cultural life of Canada (cited in Calliste 1989, 138). Department of Immigration memos suggest that Canada lost interest in the importation of Caribbean domestics even as a temporary and expedient measure when authorities calculated that the World War could result in 'better' types of immigrants.

> Canada would be adopting a very short-sighted policy to encourage the immigration of coloured people of any class or occupation. At its best it would only be a policy of expediency and it is altogether unnecessary in view of the present upheaval in Europe, which will unfortunately throw upon the labour market a large number of women of a most desirable class. (Cited in Calliste 1989, 138)

Long after the short-lived Guadeloupe domestic worker arrangement ended, the alleged 'immorality' of these women was still being used to explain the restrictions on Caribbean immigration (Mackenzie 1988, 128). Immigration of black domestic workers did not occur again until the 1950s.

In 1955, after exhausting attempts in Europe to secure domestic workers, and with mounting pressure from Caribbean governments and Britain, Canada finally entered into a domestic scheme with Jamaica and Barbados. Because the scheme involved a breach of immigration regulations in place, the government used its Order-in-Council powers to put it into effect (Mackenzie 1988, 133). Rather than acknowledging its gratitude for receiving a much needed and qualified workforce, the Canadian government reasoned that the scheme was 'a favour' to the countries of emigration. This interpretation provided a rationale for why Caribbean domestics were not eligible to apply for the interest-free loans under the 1950 Assisted Passage Loan Scheme. Significantly different from many prior Canadian foreign domestic programs, the Caribbean scheme required the sending countries to bear the responsibilities and the costs for recruiting, training, medically testing, and arranging the transportation of domestics to Canada. To qualify under the program, applicants had to be unmarried, between the ages of twenty-one and thirty-five, and willing to perform domestic work for at least one year with an assigned employer. Upon their arrival in Canada, the domestics, who had already undergone extensive medical tests, were further subjected to gynaecological examinations (Mackenzie 1988, 134–5).

Through tests for pregnancy, and the emphasis on women's single status, the Canadian government wanted to ensure that this group would be in Canada solely for the purpose of filling a labour requirement; it was assumed that there would be no sponsorship of spouses and children. Temporary migration, instead of permanent landed immigrant status, was contemplated for Caribbean domestics during the development of the scheme. However, the Canadian government decided against such a move on the grounds that it could be interpreted as a practice of forced labour and a blatant case of discrimination. The government also rejected temporary status on the assumption that, unlike European domestics, the Caribbean women would face discrimination in the labour market and thus most probably stay in domestic work past their one-year contract obligation. A third reason for the decision against temporary status was the possibility that the government could use 'administrative measures' instead of blatantly discriminatory policies to prevent domestics from 'abusing' the scheme by moving on to other occupations (Calliste 1989, 143; Mackenzie 1988, 133). In an unusual deal made with the governments of sending countries, Canada ruled that Caribbean domestics, if found unsuitable for domestic work, would be deported to the country of emigration at the expense of the Caribbean government concerned. No definition of 'unsuitable' was given in the agreement, which implied that Canadian immigration could use unlimited discretion (Daenzer 1993, 53–4).

At least initially, the Caribbean domestic scheme was considered to be the most successful of such programs initiated in the postwar period (Mackenzie 1988, 136). Canada was receiving an over-qualified work-force to perform domestic labour at no cost to itself. Many of the women recruited under the program were so highly educated that their emigra-tion contributed to a 'brain drain' from Barbados (Calliste 1989, 145). Despite their qualifications, however, Caribbean women tended to stay in domestic service longer than European domestics arriving under sim-ilar schemes (Calliste 1989, 145).

Soon after the start of the Caribbean domestic scheme, immigration officials began to raise concerns when some domestic workers made applications to sponsor relatives. To immigration authorities, the possi-bility of an 'explosion' of sponsorship, with a consequent increase in numbers of 'undesirable' immigrants, spelled an end to the usefulness of the program (Mackenzie 1988, 138). As one immigration official sur-mised,

> The one unsponsored worker may meet someone's need for a domestic ser-vant for a year or two, but the result may be ten or twenty sponsored immi-grants of dubious value to Canada and who may well cause insoluble social problems ... I am greatly concerned that we may be facing a West Indian sponsorship explosion. (Cited in Satzewich 1989, 91)

Immigration officials were also disappointed with the fact that despite the discrimination in the labour market, Caribbean domestics had a high mobility rate out of domestic service. Once again, measures were considered to ensure that immigrant domestics remained in domestic service. The deputy minister of immigration ruled against forceful tac-tics in this direction, arguing that it was 'unfair in a free market econ-omy to try to freeze anyone in a lowly occupation' (cited in Mackenzie 1988, 139). Despite the ambivalence towards the Caribbean domestic scheme, the state, fearing charges of racism from the black community in Canada and a breakdown in trade relations with Caribbean countries, continued the program until 1967, when the point system became the basis of immigration policy.

Non-Racist Immigration or 'Justified' Discrimination?
Foreign Domestic Workers under the Point System

Immigration criteria were rationalized in the 1960s to make labour market needs the explicit basis for the recruitment of immigrants. In defining labour-market needs, the point system emphasizes Canada's demand for highly educated and highly skilled immigrants, with education and skill measured in formally recognized terms. This new system has been celebrated by many as marking a liberalization of immigration policy. It has been declared as a form of recruitment which has ended discrimination on the basis of ascribed criteria such as race and sex. Ironically, however, the use of the point system has enabled the Canadian state to regulate foreign domestic workers into the most unfavourable conditions legally possible in Canadian history since the abolition of slavery.

Because the definitions of 'skill' and 'education' in modern capitalist society approach domestic work as an unskilled and 'naturally' feminine type of work, domestic workers have been unable to qualify under the point system as independent immigrants. In the 1970s, the Canadian government initiated a temporary program to bring in domestics as migrant workers, i.e., as workers lacking the freedoms and rights of citizenship or of landed immigrant status (see Bakan and Stasiulis, and Daenzer, this volume). Indeed, immigration authorities deliberately and arbitrarily lowered the points awarded to domestic servants under the system so as to ensure that domestic workers did not qualify for entry as landed immigrants. Thus, indentured status for domestic workers, which in the 1950s was considered unacceptable in a free-market economy, has become acceptable since the 1970s, and remains acceptable in the 1990s. Even though this practice is seemingly 'non-racist' and 'legitimate' within the discriminatory discourses of 'skill,' 'education,' and a potentially 'self-sustaining' immigrant, how this practice can be acceptable in an otherwise liberal democratic society should be subject to severe questioning.[4] This change has taken place at a time when it was apparent that Third World women from previously unwanted sources would constitute the major supply of foreign domestic workers in Canada for the foreseeable future.

Conclusion

Social, economic, and legal conditions of paid domestic workers are generally characterized by forms of subordination based on the gender and class status of the workers. In settler colonies such as Canada, race and ethnicity have played an important part, often over and above gender and class, in shaping the status and conditions of domestic workers. This chapter has traced the differential treatment domestic workers from different racial/ethnic backgrounds have historically received from Canadian society and the state.

While middle-class biases and paternalism formed a part of the schemes designed to bring in British domestics during the late nineteenth and early twentieth centuries, these schemes also treated immigrant domestics as 'mothers of the nation' who were welcomed to Canada as central participants in nation-building. Compared with British domestics, Scandinavian and Central and Eastern European domestic workers arriving in the early and mid-twentieth century faced linguistic and cultural disadvantages. Even though they were not recognized as full members of the Canadian nation, they were able to improve their conditions of work to the extent that they enjoyed class and ethnocultural solidarity in their respective communities. In the postwar period, as the efforts to import domestics from the preferred sources of Britain and Western Europe failed, Canada first tapped 'displaced labour' camps for East European domestic labour and then entered into 'bulk' recruitment schemes with Italy, Greece, and Spain. Employers generally treated Southern European domestics as ignorant, 'primitive villagers' who were culturally unprepared for the high standards of Canadian housekeeping. Most of these schemes were of short duration due to class, racial/ethnic, and religious biases against Southern European women and the unwillingness of the workers to put up with unfavourable working conditions.

In Canadian immigration schemes recruiting domestic workers, women of colour were considered as a last resort, when recruitment from all European sources failed. Since the late 1950s, the Caribbean, and since the mid-1970s, the Philippines have become the major source regions for foreign domestic workers. A drastic change in immigration policies coincided with the shift in source countries from Europe to the Third World. It is ironic that the recent emergence of migrant, as opposed to immigrant, status for foreign domestic workers came precisely at the time when Canada claimed to have rid its immigration policies and procedures of racial and ethnic biases. Just when Canada started to define itself as 'multicultural,' it developed policies which defined some groups of immigrants as 'workers only' (Carty 1994), disposable non-members who, despite their contributions, are given no acknowledged part in the 'nation' or 'nation-building' project. The easy acceptance by many Canadians of migrant status for foreign domestic workers may have as much to do with racial/ethnic considerations in private domestic service, as it does with the long devalued status of domestic labour in modern society.

Notes

1 The term 'inside the state' has been used by Beckett (1988) to characterize the over-regulated lives of Aboriginal people.
2 Between 1926 and 1931, even following strict procedures of selection and supervision, as much as 4.6 per cent of British female domestics were deported (cited in Valverde 1991, 127).
3 Between 1872 and 1888, female domestics along with farming families, received the most favourable fares. After 1888, responding to general opposition to assisted immigration, the government ended assisted passage and instead started to give bonuses to agents who would arrange advanced fares with employers. In the 1920s, the practices of assisted passage loans and reduced fares were started again when the Canadian government accepted the Empire Settlement Act introduced by the British government to encourage empire migration (Barber 1987; 1991, 9–10).
4 For a discussion of some of the racist, sexist, and class-based discourses justifying such treatment, see Arat-Koc (1992).

3

An Affair between Nations: International Relations and the Movement of Household Service Workers[1]

PATRICIA M. DAENZER

Introduction

The current Live-in Caregiver Program (LCP), in place since 1992, and the 1981 Foreign Domestic Movement (FDM), its predecessor, are both characterized by neocolonial features. Women from the labour forces of selected poor nations are conscripted to work under conditions that are reminiscent of indenture, in work greatly devalued by Canadians. While employed in the program, the citizenship rights of most immigrant domestic workers are limited in ways that curtail their freedom of domicile, occupational mobility, and potential for collective labour association. Most of these oppressive conditions of the occupation emerged during the post-1940s period.

Historical analysis of the LCP and FDM shows that the exploitation of immigrant domestic workers increased when non-white women were included in the program. Prior to the 1940s, the British white domestics who predominated in the program enjoyed citizenship and mobility rights upon entering Canada. The post-1940s saw an erosion of these rights during the period when most domestic workers were non-white. This chapter examines both the 1981 and 1992 policy changes, and shows that, when compared to the pre-1980s policy/program, major policy regressions were formalized in the 1981 FDM, and strengthened through the 1992 LCP. These policy regressions reinforced the most adverse aspects of the policy directly affecting working conditions and citizenship status of most domestics.

Elsewhere, contributors to this volume have argued that racial minority domestic servants, especially those from the Philippines and the

Caribbean, suffer discriminination when their experiences are compared to those of predominantly white nannies from Britain and Europe (see also Daenzer 1993; 1991; Bakan and Stasiulis 1994; 1995). It is argued here that the most regressive features of the post-1940s immigrant domestic work program are sustained by nation-to-nation agreements that link Canada and the source nations of domestic workers through the trade in female labour.

The relationship that existed between Canada and Britain in the pre-1940s with regard to domestic workers is markedly different from that which exists between Canada and current primary source/sending nations of domestic workers. The economically impoverished Philippines, which currently exports the largest number of domestic servants, and Jamaica, which exported many women in the 1970s and early 1980s, re-established with Canada a new form of colonial relationship. The commodification of female labour is the central feature of this market arrangement between these Third World nation states and Canada. This new form of colonialism, or neocolonialism, differs in form rather than substance from that discussed by authors such as Harris (1988), Bolaria and Li (1988), Sassen-Koob (1981), Calliste (1989), and Bakan (1987). Early political economic relations between developed and less developed nations were characterized by forced settlement and resource extraction, and by the subjugation of inhabitants by settlers. Neocolonialism as applied here includes the deferential consent to resource extraction and exploitation without settlement.

This neocolonialism survives because poor nations such as the Philippines benefit in certain respects from this otherwise unequal relationship with Canada. By far the greatest benefit to the Philippines is the conditional benevolence of the Canadian state in accepting the surplus female workers from their labour force, the concomitant return of financial remittances, and a relationship which yields opportunity for trade, foreign investment and aid from Canada. The victims of this affair between nations are domestic workers who enter Canadian society as indentured labour without the full protection of citizenship, symbolizing a form of 'dowry' that maintains political and economic relations with Canada. This is not unlike the relationship Canada maintains with the Caribbean; access to devalued labour in exchange for economic benefits was explicit at the onset of the postwar inclusion of Caribbean domestic workers into the program (Calliste 1991; Harris 1988; Daenzer 1991; 1993).

The argument developed below is that Canada maintains these particular neocolonial agreements because of the benefits derived for Canadian class interests. For example, the 1981 FDM was the policy outcome of recommendations made by the Task Force on Immigration Practices and Procedures struck by the minister of Employment and Immigration, Lloyd Axworthy, in 1980. In large measure, this task force was a response to the growing protest in Canada against the conditions endured by domestic workers, and the seemingly arbitrary policy measures that regulated the occupation. The mandate and impetus for this task force included a broad mission to examine the Immigration Act (1976), and specifically the process of granting employment authorizations to temporary immigrant workers. Domestic workers on temporary visas were the focus of much of this inquiry.

It is argued below that it was no accident that the nineteen recommendations listed in Appendix 1 (see p. 105), put forward by the task force in 1981, failed to address the causes of the most salient abuses known to exist in the domestic work program. The task force based its deliberations on submissions from advocates, from accounts of the unacceptable working conditions of immigrant domestic workers, and from academic and bureaucratic analyses and reports. However, the task force was overwhelmingly influenced by a prior political agenda that did not include the protection of domestics from exploitation. The analysis that follows explores this underpinning agenda, and suggests reasons why the task force opted for what they perceived to be more pragmatic and politically balanced alternatives.

In 1992, the FDM policy was again revised following lengthy internal consultations. The 1992 policy announcement naming the LCP claimed that the new educational requirement of a Canadian Grade 12 equivalent for entry into the program was an attempt to screen out the most vulnerable women, those undereducated and unskilled, from the harsh rejection of the post-domestic-work labour market (Canada, Employment and Immigration 1992, 3). Yet the acquisition of a Grade 12 education is not a sufficient condition to insulate women of colour from racism and other labour force prejudices in the Canadian labour market. Rather, the policy did just the opposite.

The 1992 policy restated aspects of the 1981 policy and reaffirmed the rescinding of citizenship and occupational mobility rights. This chapter explains why these policy regressions persist in spite of vigorous lobbying by domestic work advocacy organizations, and heightened public awareness of the conditions under which most immigrant domestic workers exist.

Finally, this chapter concludes that the exploitation of non-white domestic workers is sanctioned and managed through nation-to-nation agreements, and complements Canada's racialized labour structure and social relations. Successive policy revisions since the post-1940s period were, in sum, incremental regressions with racialized outcomes.

**The Social Construction of Class through Gender and Race:
Trends from the Earlier Domestic Work Movement**

The history of the domestic work program may be divided into two broad eras: an earlier period prior to the 1940s, and a modern or more recent period after the 1940s. The two periods are differentiated by changes in the demographic characteristics of the women who entered the program from overseas, and structural changes that correspond to these demographic ones. Until the 1940s, domestics who entered Canada were mostly British and white; they entered Canada as full citizens. After the 1940s, Eastern and Southern European women, and women of colour, previously inadmissible into the program, were then brought to Canada as domestics (Stasiulis 1990; Daenzer 1993; Calliste 1989).

Throughout the history of the domestic work program, however, two central features would remain salient. First, immigrant women would be commodified and devalued to serve class interests. This reconstruction into labour entities would be aided and abetted by the governments of sending nations. As instruments from which labour was extracted, they would be ascribed a value that corresponded to prevailing economic class domination. Second, from the pre-1940s period through to the 1990s, the state would organize the domestic service occupation to benefit elite class interests by minimizing the possibility of domestic labour conflict. Increasingly, however, and certainly by the 1970s, it was evident that notwithstanding their non-unionization, domestics could not be silenced about their oppression. The Canadian state was compelled, therefore, to engage in a process of policy manipulation in order to control domestic workers' resistance to their occupational condition. By 1981, the Canadian state formally withheld citizenship rights from immigrant domestic workers for limited durations,[2] and thus maximized the obstacles to their resistance.

Scholars who have written on the domestic work issue have postulated a servant/mistress class struggle – an affair between women in the construction and maintenance of social relations (Roberts 1979; Calliste

1991; Macklin 1992; Stasiulis 1990; Daenzer 1991; 1993). They have shown that the poverty experienced by some women in less developed nations accounts for much of the choice to enter domestic work under unsafe conditions. What remains underexplored is why national governments, fully informed about the occupational exploitation of overseas domestic work, continue to send their female citizens into labour arrangements that deny them human rights and reflect common features of class and gender subjugation.

The class, race, and gender dynamics that shaped the early history of the domestic work program in Canada are still central features today. British women are no longer brought in as future wives and procreators, but white British nannies are still preferred as domestics in the program.[3] Immigrant domestic workers still function as instruments of private wealth and international market commodities. The Canadian state plays a central role in the location and occupational status-definition of these immigrant servants. Sending nations benefit through market affiliation with Canada and from the remittances sent home by domestic workers. And, far from being passive subjects in this nation-to-nation arrangement, the women have their own vested interests in variously defined forms of status mobility.

The current class conflict evident in the mistress/servant relationship, made complex by the added issues of citizenship and race, is, then, the social outcome of an affair between nations. This class-based competition among women – mistresses versus servants – vying for ascendancy in the Canadian marketplace is the manifestation of a national domestic workers' policy fostered by the Canadian state. It is nurtured internationally by nations eager to benefit from the export of their female citizens to a more lucrative labour market.

Four historical episodes of the program illustrate this pattern. The early British domestic movement phase prior to the 1940s was seen to be more than a labour-market strategy. The movement of white British women to Canada under a domestic work program was a nation-to-nation strategy for the strengthening and continuity of the white race in Canada (Roberts 1979). The early movement also benefited Britain's economy by exporting surplus female labour to the developing Canadian colony. In addition, the importation of, and ready access to, a 'servant class' also enhanced status definition with additional benefits of low-cost accumulation for upper-class British settlers. The legacy of the pre-1940s movement holds programmatic significance for developments in the post-1940s period. White British servants would continue to be preferred and ascribed a status above women of colour and Eastern and Southern European women. The preference for white and British childminders in Canadian homes relates to the (Anglo-Saxon) Canadian link to British heritage (Bakan and Stasiulis 1995) and the predisposition towards white domination. The explicit pre-1940s aim of nation-building and racial preservation remains politically relevant, although it is now expressed in cultural terms through a preference for white nannies.

The second historical episode of significance is the movement of war-displaced persons (DPs) from Eastern and Southern Europe following World War Two. The agreement to accept war-displaced persons into Canada was urged by the International Labour Organization (ILO) and by public criticism against Canadian reluctance in joining in the refugee emigration scheme (Daenzer 1993). Even then, Canada's subsequent agreement to join in the movement of displaced persons was formalized only after the economic benefits had been calculated through extensive province-to-province negotiations. The 1947 Canada-European agreement to relieve Europe of persons economically and socially displaced by the war, resulted in the relocation of carefully screened refugees into positions of indenture as domestic workers on Canadian farms, in institutions, and in private homes. Objections to the terms of this relocation and consequent exploitation were raised by Germany in the 1950s.

The third notable nation-to-nation episode in the history of the domestic work movement was the inclusion of black Caribbean domestic workers in 1955. Responding to internal and overseas pressures to soften the racist exclusionary aspects of Canadian immigration, Canada struck a deal with Caribbean authorities in exchange for admitting a small number of black women into positions of domestic work (Calliste 1989; 1991; Harris 1988; Brand 1991; Stasiulis 1990; Satzewich 1992; 1993; Daenzer 1991; 1993). The Caribbean women were to be admitted under special arrangements, agreed to by Caribbean officials, which included the denial of mobility rights, excessive monitoring, and less remuneration than other domestics. In exchange for this access of Caribbean women into the program, Canadian officials reasoned that Canada would thus be able to improve trade and political relations with the Caribbean region.

Finally, like the Caribbean episode, the entry of Filipino women into Canada was due to a compromise struck between the government of Canada and the Philippines. Reacting to Canadian and American classification of Filipino (Asian) citizens as an inadmissible class of immigrants, the Philippines threatened reciprocal sanctions against the entry of Canadian and American business immigrants in the 1960s.

> The Department was informed by External Affairs that the Philippine Congress had under consideration a bill entitled 'The Reciprocal Immigration Bill' ... designed to ensure that no alien would be admitted to the Philippines unless he could prove that Filipinos were not prevented by legislation ... from entering or residing in the alien's country.[4]

In order to gain access to the Filipino labour and resource market, Canadian authorities amended immigration procedures to remove Filipino citizens from the list of inadmissible aliens. The subsequent easing of immigration restrictions both by the Philippines and by Canada benefited the two nations. Filipino women began entering the Canadian domestic work occupation at a time when it was increasingly difficult to attract sufficient numbers of women from other nations into the occupation. Canadian entrepreneurs were able to access the expansive Filipino market and also benefit from their labour at devalued rates.

The domestic work program in its current form grew out of these arrangements and compromises between nation states. The transactions between state authorities across borders was, however, only the beginning of the economic, social, and political construction of this servant class of women. The historical episodes discussed above are significant for understanding why Canada has been able to subjugate and exploit immigrant domestic workers with impunity. These episodes also shed light on the collusive silence of the 'sending' or source nations, with regard to the exploitation and abuse of the rights of their citizens.

An enduring feature of the program was to be the intransigence of policy makers in Canada in refusing to initiate reforms in spite of years of advocacy aimed at humanizing the domestic work occupation and gaining modest protection for female domestics. Central to the concerns that advocates had been raising was the growing trend by the Department of Employment and Immigration of denying landed immigrant status to domestics who originated from the Caribbean and the Philippines. The denial of landed immigrant status to women of colour led to other social and personal abuses.

By the late 1970s it was evident that Employment and Immigration could no longer afford to be perceived as ignoring these growing protests. The Federal Government established a task force to inquire into the situation of 'Foreign Domestic Workers on Employment Authorizations.' The dynamics during and following the report of the task force provide evidence that the Canadian state was driven by concerns for meeting the economic and social needs of Canada's wealthy at the expense of the 'immigrant servant class' they had constructed over the last half-century. The policy that resulted from the task force exercise showed that Employment and Immigration negated any obligation to protect the interests of immigrant domestics, but instead was compelled to serve its wealthy 'client group' to the best of its ability.

The Limits of Obligation: Between State, Women, and Servants

In September 1980, the new minister of Employment and Immigration, Lloyd Axworthy, commissioned a Task Force on Immigration Practices and Procedures with a mandate to assess the degree of confluence between the Immigration Act 1976 and immigration procedures, with emphasis on workers on employment authorizations. The guiding principles of the task force were (a) to protect the interests of Canada, and, (b) to achieve fairness in the treatment of individuals (Canada, Employment and Immigration 1980). In November 1981, the task force submitted its report, *Domestic Workers on Employment Authorizations*, to the minister. It stated what had been known for nearly a half-century: that immigrant domestic workers on employment authorizations were severely disadvantaged and abused through their occupational arrangement.

In spite of informed consultations and lengthy deliberations about the exploitation known to be prevalent in the occupation, the nineteen recommendations ultimately downplayed or indeed nullified the reports of abuses. Instead, the task force put forward a policy framework that contradicted its own discussions and suggestions. In their discussions they acknowledged, for example, that 'there have been sufficient reports of mistreatment [of domestic workers] to focus public attention on their plight and their particular vulnerability to abuse' (Canada, Employment and Immigration 1980, 12).

Six of those recommendations are of particular relevance to this discussion. In these six recommendations, listed below, the task force acknowledged the need for measures to address the sources of the exploitation endured by domestic workers. In other recommendations (listed in Appendix 1), the task force attempted to balance the competing interests of Canadian employers and immigrant domestic workers through ineffective proposals.

Task Force Recommendation no. 2:
There should be no restriction on the number of renewals of temporary employment authorizations given to a domestic worker, provided there is no justifiable reason for not renewing it.

Task Force Recommendation no. 5:
Upon receipt of a confirmed offer of employment, a domestic worker should be processed for permanent residence in Canada, and should be permitted to come to Canada on a temporary employment authorization. The application for permanent residence should be approved within a year of the applicant taking employment in Canada, provided there is no justifiable reason for refusing the application, as defined by Sections 19 and 27 of the Immigration Act (a system similar to that presently in operation for entrepreneurial applications).

Task Force Recommendation no. 6:
In recognition of the high demand for domestic workers in Canada, applications for permanent residence should be accorded full points under the Occupational Demand category of the selection criteria (schedule 1, Immigration Regulations). Domestic workers should be reclassified under the category vocational preparation, in recognition of the variety of tasks performed and skills needed. They should be assessed in category (e) where the amount of training required is twelve months or more and less than two years.

Task Force Recommendation no. 12:
A domestic worker should be able to change employers without jeopardizing her status in Canada.

Task Force Recommendation no. 14:
Given the significant number of temporary workers in Canada, the Government of Canada should sign the International Labour Conference's Convention #143 'concerning migrations into abusive conditions and the promotion of equality of opportunity and treatment of migrant workers.'

Task Force Recommendation no. 15:
Establishment of legislation covering wages and working conditions of domestic workers on temporary employment authorizations should be immediately drafted and introduced into the House of Commons, in accordance with the policy of the Liberal Party in Opposition and following the

precedent established by the Caribbean and Mexican Seasonal Agricultural Workers' Program.

What then would have motivated the task force to propose such recommendations, which apparently offered greater protection to these migrant women workers? In deliberating the competing interests of the Canadian state and its middle-class Canadian clientele against those of non-Canadian domestics, the task force yielded to political pragmatism. In moving from recommendations to policy, the task force negated the rights of migrant domestic workers – those without landed immigrant status. It was simple to deny rights to this group; they were women without the protection of state-masters and therefore vulnerable to political and social abuses. There was, after all, an understanding between sending nations and Canada about the limits of obligation within the contractual arrangement which permitted women, at least in theory, to 'queue-jump' access into Canada through the domestic work loophole. The task force therefore reflected and legitimated the limited obligations of the Canadian state regarding the interests of non-white female foreign workers.

During their deliberations, the task force cited the tension between domestic workers' tenuous immigration status and the significance of landed immigrant status in mediating their vulnerability. The absence of landed immigrant status was a bureaucratically imposed obstacle. Landed status is granted to those selected by Employment and Immigration for permanent residence in Canada, and embodies many of the rights to which other Canadians are entitled. Chief among these would be the right to choose where they live, and the right to change occupations that they found to be oppressive. What was required was a decision to grant landed status to all domestics. This would have enabled them to enter Canada with rights essential for their protection. In addition, the granting of pre-entry landed status would have the effect of redistributing power from federal employment counsellors and Canadian employers toward domestic workers.

Under the procedures of the 1981 FDM, domestic workers were treated differently from immigrants in the normal stream in other ways. The former underwent a post-entry evaluation for suitability for life in Canada; this occurred following the period of labour indenture in domestic work in Canada. Acting as gatekeepers, Manpower counsellors were given ultimate discretion in formulating perceptions about the job performance and economic stability of domestic workers who wished to remain in Canada (Canada, Employment and Immigration 1981, 13–14). They were free to judge when infractions such as deserting abusive employers and working conditions, or being fired, were grounds for deportation from Canada (Canada, Employment and Immigration 1981, 12). And since most domestic workers left the occupation following their term of indenture, the post-job assessment of the employment suitability of the domestic appeared on the surface to be useless. The post-employment assessment only minimally related to the occupation; it was rather a process of sorting and distributing surplus labour resources between Canada and the sending nations.

The post-employment assessment, then, had a more significant function. The political undertaking of entrenching or denying workers within the Canadian nation as ultimate citizen-consumers of rights and resources, was the process really attended to by manpower/employment counsellors. The value of the post-employment assessment was its potential for constructing a culturally subjective 'screening-out' process for domestics found to be undesirable for Canadian society. It was this state-maintenance task of finding 'suitable' citizens for Canada that the task force would really address through their recommendations. To them, the question was not how policies should change to affect greater fairness and justice for immigrant (non-citizen) servants. It was instead, how should Canada ensure that immigrants selected for permanent residence were those most deserving of all that Canada has to offer, and the most suited for integration into Canadian society? But a second and implied concern was at the core of their deliberations; how can Canada continue to serve the interests of influential Canadians while purporting to redress domestic exploitation? Faced with these competing needs and influences, the task force engaged in an incongruous process of deliberations that led to contradictions in their recommendations. It was not surprising that many of their ruminations gave the impression that they were seriously considering the plight of domestic workers. For example:

> It would be unpalatable simply to allow employers to propose the contract terms without any guidance from federal standards ... The Federal government has no power to become involved in regulating contracts between landed immigrants and their employers. However, where the employment authorization exists, the opportunity is available to have at least some level of involvement. (Canada, Employment and Immigration 1981, 81, 95)

They discussed four alternatives that would, at best, tinker with the existing policy without altering the substantive impact of Canada's immigration policy for procuring off-shore labour for low-skilled jobs.

In our view, it would be useful to survey the following range of policy options in relation to foreign domestic employees.

1. Deny entry altogether, either as permanent residents or on employment authorizations.
2. Restrict entry to 'landed' immigrants only.
3. Restrict entry to employment authorization only.
4. A continued combination of 2 and 3 but with modifications to present procedures.

(Canada, Employment and Immigration 1981, 81)

Had they been serious about the first alternative, they might have empowered the occupation by inducing the inclusion of domestic work on the list of occupational shortages that Canada acknowledges for immigration purposes. The continuation of 'special' immigrant movements into household service work removed the occupation from the normal Canadian labour market and blunted market scarcity, which influences wages and working conditions. In the absence of a special movement of immigrants into the domestic labour pool, employers would have been forced to be competitive by (hopefully) paying appropriate wages, since the occupation would have been open to Canadians with citizenship status. Past experience, however, had indicated that Canadian citizens or permanent residents traditionally rejected domestic work. There was, therefore, the risk that the domestic market would be filled by illegal immigrants. The latter, according to members of the task force, would be subject to even more abuses (Canada, Employment and Immigration 1981, 81). The domestic work occupation, under existing policy at the time, seems to have attracted unknown numbers of illegal immigrants. This reality was unacknowledged during the discussions by the task force.

The second alternative, the restriction of entry to landed immigrants, reflects the notion that all workers ought to have access to citizenship entitlements regardless of the tenure of their residence in Canada. The admission of all domestics as landed immigrants would have represented a return to rights previously enjoyed in the pre-1940s era. This would also have placed household service workers on an equal entry footing with other labour market immigrants. Most significantly, the system of indenture would have been replaced by relative equality of access to the Canadian labour market. This was the alternative that would have most benefited immigrant domestic workers and shifted the balance of advantages that favoured employers and the Canadian state. The task force was persuasive in its deliberations over the merit of this alternative, but would ultimately rule it out.

> In our view, the most desirable approach is to rely on the market ... On the other hand, an employer who has made an offer and waited through the landing process may legitimately complain if the person leaves after only a short time. (Canada, Employment and Immigration 1981, 89)

> We would suggest that officials advise people that generally, the authorizations would not be renewed beyond two or three years ... It would be ... fair to require landing for a prolonged stay. (Canada, Employment and Immigration 1981, 91)

On its own, however, this alternative lacked the force to change the conditions under which domestics were employed. Other measures would still be necessary to protect this class of workers from the effects of the unregulated domestic work market system. Without these, the absence of mobility out of the occupation would continue to operate as the regulator of household service working conditions. More important, this alternative would have met the needs of immigrant domestics without addressing the more important goal of the Canadian state. If occupation in domestic work was to be the sole condition of entry into Canada, it would have negated the oldest priority of immigration policy; to settle in Canada only those 'selected' and found to be most fitting and deserving. In the final analysis, it would have granted residence, and thus access to citizenship, to foreigners without their subjection to the selection process that is the reserve of the Canadian state as the receiving nation.

The third alternative, to continue admitting domestics as non-immigrants, was an adherence to the paternalism evident in the process of the colonization of immigrant women's labour. It was the alternative which would preserve the balance of power in Canada's favour and one which would serve the short-term interests of Canadian employers. This alternative would have regulated both social status and privilege and at the same time controlled access to citizenship rights within the Canadian state. It would serve to fill crucial labour gaps with limited obligations for the security of the labour pool in question.

Admitting domestics as non-immigrants would also meet the needs of source or sending nations. Access to the program for women who would not otherwise meet immigration criteria, would have ensured sending nations' access to Canadian economic resources in the form of remittances sent home by domestic workers. Sending nations would also benefit by the timely release of workers to Canada's work force – workers who might otherwise have been dependent upon their states for support. And finally, sending nations would have obtained access to Canada's labour market without the uncertainty inherent in the more rigid immigrant selection criteria. It was this programmatic option which would form the basis of both the FDM and the LCP into the 1990s.

During their deliberations, the task force was consistent in its critique of the undervaluing of the occupation of domestic work and of domestic workers. They drew attention to the point system[5] of the 1976 Immigration Act, which was seen to be particularly problematic for domestics wishing to obtain landed immigrant status.

> The arbitrarily low value set on domestics' work, particularly with children, is highly questionable ... Applicants for landing are given no points in category 4 (occupational demand). (Canada, Employment and Immigration 1981, 21)

> It cannot be stressed enough that this issue of domestics must be seen in its wider context. Domestic workers are underpaid because domestic work ... is seriously undervalued. Short term solutions must be found. Among them is finding substitutes for our least well-paid domestic workers – those on employment authorizations ... [W]e must still press for quality substitutes, and ... resist the impetus of mere 'market forces' toward plentiful, low quality, day care institutions. (Canada, Employment and Immigration 1981, 96)

Other immigrants destined for the Canadian labour force received points for occupational demand, skill and training level, and assured employment. Domestics, it was observed, were assessed differently; they were not credited for their occupational knowledge and training. In the 1960s, for example, immigration and employment officials arbitrarily diminished the value of domestic work by lowering its Occupational Demand value.[6] Thus, domestic work was subjected to fluctuating bureaucratic attitudes and biases. What, then, was a reasonable direction for the task force, given that the domestic work occupation was driven by its legacy of nation-to-nation agreements, Canadian middle-class interests, and a gatekeeping tradition steeped in racism? The recommendations suggest that the task force chose to protect Canadian state and middle-class interests and thus trivialize the oppression of domestic workers. Chief among the interests that the task force enshrined for Canada was the right to gatekeeping and immigrant population selection.

The Tradition of Gatekeeping: Regulating Access to Citizenship

Beginning in April 1981, the minister of Employment and Immigration, Lloyd Axworthy, and his departmental officials announced policy changes in the domestic work program that ignored most of the already ineffectual recommendations of the task force. Thereafter, domestics would depend on the benevolence of their employers, and on the discretion of federal government employment counsellors for adjustments to their tenuous labour status.

Of the nineteen recommendations that came from the task force, the minister's announcement reflected two of particular significance. First, domestic workers would continue to enter Canada on employment authorizations and therefore as non-immigrants. Instead of the one-year authorization period suggested by the task force, a two-year period, with assessments at one-year intervals, was announced. Extensions to their non-immigrant work permits were not to be unlimited (as per recommendation no. 2). Beyond the two-year period, extensions were only to be granted to those who would ultimately be deported. Second, domestics were to be awarded an additional ten points for their occupation. This increase in points for their occupational training would mean that some domestics would gain enough points to enter Canada as full landed immigrants.

The artificial lowering of the vocational value of domestic work and the entry into Canada of domestics as non-immigrants are mutually dependent: both features are based on racially driven selection criteria. The bureaucratically manipulated fluctuations in the occupational demand value remain central to the occupational status ascription process of non-white immigrant domestic workers. Some Immigration officials had been wary of the practice and had sounded periodic cautions: '[When] the demand for domestics dropped from 15 to 12, and the interview level was raised to 45, we were immediately concerned over the political implications.'[7]

Because the mandate of the task force included attention to 'fairness,' it was considered imperative to address the issue of exploitation that was so elaborately discussed. The minister directed action on the recommendation to have employers sign contracts that specified the terms and working conditions of their domestic servants. This procedure reflected no serious attention to exploitation, however. The policy stated that employers who violated the terms of the employment contract were to be denied future domestic workers through the program. But Employment and Immigration held no powers to deny Canadians access from sponsoring other women for live-in care regardless of their record of working conditions. This 1981 policy requirement was an empty gesture on several counts. Not only was the federal government not constitutionally empowered to enforce contracts in provincial jurisdictions and in private homes, but also it could not restrict the hiring of private employees. Without monitoring and enforcement of their status and conditions, domestic workers lacked meaningful protection.

Under the 1981 policy announcements, gatekeepers to the Canadian labour market retained maximum power in admitting foreign-born women as domestics into the country. Those workers who had served the two to three years in Canada's domestic work occupation and who were subsequently found undesirable as immigrants were to be returned to their countries of origin.[8] Attempts were made to soften the edges of the purely extractive potential of the program by an appearance of a meritorious system of vocational assessment and crediting. Yet, the phrasing of the 1981 policy guideline on the assessment of vocational preparation encouraged highly subjective judgments and highly discretionary treatment.[9] The class conflict between domestics and their employers was magnified by this aspect of the policy.

Through these policy revisions, Employment and Immigration initiated complex bureaucratization that served only to obscure the lack of regulation in the program. This facade of administrative fairness did, however, serve a useful purpose for the Canadian state. It distracted public attention away from the lack of governmental intervention to protect domestic workers from class and racial exploitation.[10]

Behind the facade, however, administrative tinkering with the entry requirements was not advantageous for many domestics workers; only a small percentage continued to enter Canada as landed immigrants. Between 1982 and 1985, the years immediately following the enactment of the FDM, only 8,029 household service workers were admitted as landed immigrants,[11] compared with 54,512 on employment authorizations (non-landed status).[12]

Other statistics bring to light the racialization of the program. During 1985, for example, 71.5 per cent of British domestic workers entered Canada as landed immigrants, compared with 53.3 per cent of domestics from the Philippines.[13]

Instead of a system based on rights for domestic workers as legitimate members of Canada's work force, the minister's 1981 announcement approved a process that would grant conditional rewards for time served in an occupation that Canadian workers had historically rejected. Occupational benefits and privileges extended to domestics were couched in provisional language, prone to highly subjective criteria, and based on unenforceable contracts. In return for being 'good' workers, they would be granted considerations from Employment and Immigration officials, and, hopefully, from their employers. These considerations could lead to changes in their status from non-immigrant economic entities to immigrants. To attain this status, four general sets of circumstances had to prevail: (1) employers had to be benevolent enough to grant time off and financial support for skills training; (2) employment counsellors had to show compassion in responding to reported cases of abuse and job loss; (3) immigration counsellors had to exercise generosity in defining the terms, 'personal suitability, adaptation, and self-sufficiency'; and (4) immigration officials and employment counsellors would be required to subordinate interdepartmental tensions to effective and equitable outcomes during the two-to-three-year process of assessment and processing of domestic workers.[14]

Employers had significant input into defining immigrant desirability and thus the power imbalance established by this expectation weighed heavily against the domestic workers' status in Canada. Her chances of becoming a self-sufficient landed immigrant in Canada depended largely upon the willingness of the employer to extend time off for the upgrading classes (three hours each week), and a contribution of $20, a rather picayune token toward this upgrading. Since employers had a vested interest in containing domestics as non-immigrants and thus occupationally immobile, the policy was clearly aimed at regulating the labour demand rather than protecting non-immigrant domestics. Data shows that most non-immigrants were non-white women (Daenzer 1993). Thus, this policy directive also had racist implications.

Benevolent Duplicity: The Construction of Servant Objects and Female Subjects

The 1981 policy announcements granted domestic workers procedural rights only; there were no substantive changes to their immigrant, and thus occupational, status. The procedural right to 'apply' for landed immigrant status from within Canada was largely nullified by the substantive exploitation, obstacles, and discretionary authority by employers and state officials that continued to characterize domestic work. For the majority of non-white domestic workers, entry into Canada's workforce as de facto citizens during the first two to three years of residency was still an illusive privilege.

In 1983, The International Coalition to End Domestic Exploitation (INTERCEDE), based in Toronto and acting as the main advocacy group for domestic workers, rated the policy changes stemming from the 1981 announcement as less than satisfactory and made thirty-five recommendations for moving toward a policy that would institutionalize certain rights for domestic workers of non-immigrant status (INTERCEDE 1983).

Domestic work applicants, however, had more rights than were obvious. In 1985 the Federal Court of Canada ruled that the 'self-sufficiency' criterion of the premigration assessment for temporary domestics was illegal. A person seeking a temporary work authorization, suggested the judicial system, could not be assessed on criteria that related to 'the potential for long-term establishment.'[15] In other words, the courts agreed that Canada could continue to exercise the tradition of selective gatekeeping, by admitting only those who are perceived to have the right amount of productive potential and social appropriateness. The point established by the court ruling, however, is that in the case of domestic workers on non-immigrant visas, this particular selection criterion was inappropriate. Why was this?

Immigration officials were being challenged by the courts to pay attention to the very issue they had ignored following the task force's recommendations – to establish whether domestic workers were indeed 'working visitors' to be deported at the end of their work contract, or, if they were, in fact, 'residents.' If they were working visitors, then immigration bureaucrats neither had the right nor the need to regulate status ascription merely by interpreting aspirant immigrants' potential as citizens. On the other hand, if they were residents, then they ought to be admitted in the same manner as other residents – following assessment and selection, with full landed immigrant status with its attendant occupational mobility and other rights.

Had the court ruling been taken seriously, it would not have been possible for Employment and Immigration to continue to operate the domestic work program in the shadow of such benevolent duplicity. As operationalized, the policy appeared to be 'kind' to domestic workers by promising them the reward of 'potential citizenship' at the end of their indenture. It was, in fact, an improvement upon the pre-1981 practice of containing domestics as non-landed immigrants in perpetuity. But, according to the courts, the immigration procedure of processing domestic workers as both immigrants and visitors was a violation of its own legal framework. Even though these challenges to the system of exploiting selected domestic workers would lead to another policy review in 1985, Employment and Immigration chose to ignore the court's ruling.

> We do not think that it is the job of the courts to establish the substantive criteria to be employed in the selection of foreign domestics nor do we believe that the courts have any particular competence to do so. As long as the FDM program continues to rest on its current inadequate legal base, and as long as our present selection criteria remain as nebulous as they are, we shall, however, be inviting the courts to continue to establish the selection criteria for us.[16]

The nation-to-nation agreements that institutionalized the exploitative traffic of women into domestic work were to continue.

Consequently, in 1987, the 1985 policy review resulted in a reiteration of the central features of the 1981 policy. This time, however, it clarified in writing aspects of the program that were previously vague and discretionary: domestics could, with permission, change jobs to escape abuses; domestics could live out if employers consented; domestics would not necessarily be deported for living out.[17]

Some domestic workers, however, were still essentially commodities serving labour needs of sending and receiving nations. And, ultimately, non-immigrant domestic workers were considered permanent citizens only of their nations of origin. Therefore, as long as sending nations consented to this collusive trade in female labour, which earned them favours with Canada, the dominant characteristics of the domestic work occupation would steadfastly guide relations between its incumbent women and their states. A summary of the 1987 guidelines reveals this pattern:

- Domestics were still required to live in the homes of their employers, but could, with the consent of the employer, opt to live out without penalty.
- Domestics were still to enter Canada without full status as landed immigrants.
- Domestics were restricted to household service work.
- Domestics could not change employment without the permission of Employment and Immigration officials; the previous arrangement by which employers also had to consent to this change in writing, was later discontinued in 1986.
- Domestics were required to report job loss.
- Officials would exercise judgment regarding whether domestics had lost their employment 'through no fault of their own.'
- Officials were empowered to 'forgive' minor violations committed by domestics. Living out, or apart from the employer, was such a violation.
- Domestics had to prove that they could manage their finances.
- Domestics were required to report community contacts or activities; these formed the basis of assessment.[18]

In the final analysis, the new policy directive clearly stated: '[It] is the individual immigration officer's assessment, based on all the factors and information which is considered relevant, of the domestic's actual or potential successful establishment and self-sufficiency which will determine approval or refusal of landing.'[19]

The fact that the domestic work policy persisted in spite of its legal tenuousness was not surprising.[20] Employment and Immigration officials were instructed to exercise caution but to continue discretion in the rationing of Canadian membership to women who were categorized as time-limited labour resources. The agreements between Canada and nations that subscribed to the domestic work program were simply for the supply of occupationally specific labour. Any benefits that might accrue to the women were to be discretionary and in Canada's interest. Officials of Canada Immigration Centres (CICs) continued to have the ultimate say as gatekeepers for issuing work permits and determining immigration status:

> There may be occasions where domestics who were refused landing by CICs because they had failed to demonstrate sufficient ability to establish in Canada, reapply ... at visa offices once their three year term is concluded. Officers should ... bear in mind the CICs decision that the domestic has not demonstrated a propensity for successful establishment. In view of this it is unlikely that a visa officer would reach a contrary decision.[21]

By 1989, another departmental review of the FDM was under way. Also in 1989, INTERCEDE conducted a survey into the status and experience of domestics and made recommendations for further policy changes. INTERCEDE showed that by the end of the 1980s, domestics were still largely unremunerated for overtime work; cases of sexual harassment of domestics by some employers were reported, and linked to the requirement to live in the employer's home; alienation from the larger community was still a problem for domestics; and workers continued to be denied rights such as choice over living conditions and adequate food (INTERCEDE 1989, 3–10) (see Appendix 2, p. 107).

The policy review initiated in 1989 clarified minor ambiguities in a changed policy announced in 1992 entitled The Live-in Caregiver Program (LCP), which replaced the FDM. The new policy reiterated that domestics in the program would continue to live in their employers homes, and enter Canada as non-immigrants. The minister's announcement said:

> The new program responds to concerns expressed by employers, domestic workers and their representatives over the course of the extensive review of the former program. I am confident that the new requirements will ensure that those who participate in the Live-in Caregiver Program have the skills and experience to meet labour market demands. (Canada, Employment and Immigration 1992b, 1)

The stricter educational requirements of the LCP meant that domestics had to provide evidence that they had completed the equivalent of a Canadian Grade 12 education, and also six months of formal training in household service work. The 1992 announcement also officially removed the requirement that domestic workers obtain letters of release from their employers before changing jobs, thus removing an odious symbol of their indentured status. Changing employers still required the permission of Employment and Immigration, however. Domestics were advised that they had sole responsibility for monitoring the contracts they signed with employers; Employment and Immigration still had no jurisdiction to enforce employer/employee contracts (Canada, Employment and Immigration 1992b, 4).

The 1992 policy also eliminated one specific and troublesome form of domestic workers' dependency on their employers, initiated through the previous requirement for upgrading in the 1981 policy. Since domestics would now have to have qualifications for 'self-sufficiency' in order to be eligible for entering the program, employers were no longer required to grant time off and an allowance for upgrading.

The 1992 policy politically entrenched the most adverse aspects of the domestic work program. Trends that had been evolving incrementally since the 1940s were solidified. The policy showed that Canada could, if it so desired, limit the citizenship rights of newcomers. The ambiguities pertaining to the rights of migrant servants versus the rights of Canadian women/employers were also resolved in this policy. The policy placed the needs of Canadian employers above the rights of their migrant women servants, through the insistence on the live-in requirement. Since it was assumed that Canadian employers wanted servants to live in their homes, this was the sole condition under which foreign women could enter Canada to work as domestics.

Between 1982 and 1990, more than 67,000 domestics were admitted to Canada under the FDM.[22] Regional shifts in source countries are most evident in the 1980s. In contrast to the 1940s and 1950s when the majority of domestics were British or European, by 1989 50 per cent of domestics originated in the Philippines (46 per cent in 1988 and 49.6 per cent in 1989). Only 9.4 per cent of domestics originated in Britain in 1988, and just over 8 per cent in 1989.[23]

The domestic workers of the 1980s and early 1990s enjoyed fewer substantive rights than those of the 1940s and 1950s. The withdrawal of citizenship rights from the more recent non-white domestic workers intensified the level of exploitation they endured under the post-1980s program. Yet, none of the source nations from which domestic workers originated have raised public objections over the well-documented exploitation of their citizens since the 1970s. The practice of exporting female workers who filled labour gaps in Canada and concurrently supplemented their national economies through remittances remains a quiet process of benevolent duplicity between nations.

Conclusion: Political and Economic Commodification of Immigrant Female Labour

The postwar era has seen four decades of advocacy by domestic workers to improve their condition, which is state-managed by a top-heavy Canadian federal government bureaucracy. Yet despite these efforts, over the last four decades domestic workers have lost occupational privileges, while other workers have benefited from incremental improvements to their working conditions. The regression in rights within the domestic work occupation (loss of landed immigrant status, loss of mobility rights) occurred following two major reviews that had 'fairness' as central aims. This regression in rights also emphasizes the racialization of the occupation whereby women of colour have replaced white women. Yet, sending nations have been silent on the issue of the exploitation of their citizens. Their silence maintains economic and political relations with Canada.

The minister's statement of April 1992 reconfirmed that the LCP was an affair between Canada and sending nations: 'The Live-In Caregiver Program exists only because there is a shortage of Canadians to fill the need for live-in care work' (Canada, Employment and Immigration 1992a). Canada required the partnership of other nations to address this labour-market need. For more than a half-century, Canada had found it impossible to structure this occupation in ways deemed desirable by Canadian workers. This particular form of labour, then, could only be met by entering into agreements with nations that benefited from such a contract. In this affair between Canada and its 'labour supplier' nations, domestic workers had to be located in a particular context without the capability of resisting this location. This was the reiteration of the 1992 policy. It reinforced for affluent Canadian families rights over immigrant live-in servants, and concurrently enforced obligations on sending nations to supply only labour trained at their expense. None of this was new; a comparison of the pre- and post-1940s periods reveals that domestic workers were commodified to serve the interests of sending states, Canada's privileged class, and the Canadian state.

In addition, the postwar history of the domestic work policy shows that the opening up of the program to non-whites began a five-decade season of manipulation of the policy to regulate non-white domestic workers into a marginalized working-class category. Faced with the continued 'demand' from Canada for commodified workers in the form of female foreign domestics, sending nations continue to provide the 'supply'; the market in domestic workers continues even in conditions of tightening borders and restricted rights.

Although some relationship exists between the domestic work program and concerns regarding child-care availability in Canada, the 1992 policy was more focused on restricting the ability of Third World women to enter Canada as domestic workers than on responding to welfare needs. Recent government statistics confirm that a radical decline in the number of foreign domestics has occurred since the LCP was put into effect. The total number of entrants who acquired employment authorizations to work as foreign domestics in Canada fell from 8,630 in 1991 to 1,866 in 1995. In terms of women from the historically major Third World source countries, the figures are stark. Those entering from the Philippines declined from 5,493 in 1993 to 1,392 in 1995; from the English-speaking Caribbean (Jamaica, Trinidad-Tobago, Barbados, Bahamas, Grenada, and St Vincent), the numbers declined from 379 to 21.[24] As demand for live-in care has in no way declined – indications are that it has, in fact, increased – the tighter restrictions on the legal entry of Third World women lends credence to the suspicion that the LCP has increased the illegal market in domestic workers.

The post-1970s increase in Canadian women into paid labour outside the home resulted in greater demands for child care, but the domestic work program goes beyond this. Historically, middle-class women and affluent families have found the live-in arrangement of the domestic work program convenient to their life styles and needs. The increased advocacy against the subjugation of domestics heightened at a time when many middle-class women were quite dependent upon the program to support their own occupational and status mobility. For professional women with young children, career advancement was also dependent upon child-care provision. Eliminating the live-in requirement would have been an affront to the privilege of middle-class women. Thus, the 1992 policy was also the state's public affirmation of the preservation of class privileges. Economic interests have been, and continue to be, the primary considerations that guided the opening up of the program to non-British and to non-white women.

Canadian officials have conceded, over repeated policy reviews, that the domestic work program reflected one aspect of international economic interdependence between nations; the indispensability of this arrangement between nations has thus been affirmed.[25] This interdependence is sustained by nation states through economic and political commodity exchange. Domestic workers are essential political links for poorer nations wishing economic relations with Canada. For Canadian households, domestic workers have long been an economic resource unattainable locally. Domestic workers can only materialize as a benefit within this process of commodification if they are silenced by limitations to their citizenship status.

Appendix 1 Recommendations of 'Domestic Workers on Employment Authorizations: A Report on the Task Force on Immigration Practices and Procedures' (1981)

1. Instructions should be immediately issued to the field officers to assess applications for permanent residence by domestic workers who have resided continuously in Canada for a reasonable period of time, on the basis of success in establishing themselves in Canada. This should be the sole criterion by which such applications are assessed.

2. There should be no restriction on the number of renewals of temporary employment authorizations given to a domestic worker, provided there is no justifiable reason for not renewing it.

3. The pamphlet 'Working Temporarily in Canada – Facts for Foreign Workers,' should be revised to explain the Regulations covering spouse and dependent children of temporary visa workers in Canada. Immigration officers should be required to advise the temporary worker of the Regulations presently in existence.

4. Domestic workers presently in Canada on valid employment authorizations should be permitted to apply for permanent residence from within the country, and should be assessed on the basis of their present or potential successful establishment in Canada.

5. Upon receipt of a confirmed offer of employment, a domestic worker should be processed for permanent residence in Canada, and should be permitted to come to Canada on a temporary employment authorization. The application for permanent residence should be approved within a year of the applicant taking employment in Canada, provided there is no justifiable reason for refusing the application, as defined by Sections 19 and 27 of the Immigration Act (a system similar to that presently in operation for entrepreneurial applications).

6. In recognition of the high demand for domestic workers in Canada, applications for permanent residence should be accorded full points under the Occupational Demand category of the selection criteria

(schedule 1, Immigration Regulations). Domestic workers should be reclassified under the category vocational preparation, in recognition of the variety of tasks performed and skills needed. They should be assessed in category (e) where the amount of training required is twelve months or more and less than two years.

7. Before a confirmation of an offer of employment may be sent to a domestic worker, an employer should be required to sign a legally-enforceable contract, setting out the terms and conditions of employment, which will be signed by the domestic worker before she begins to work. This can be facilitated by sending the contract.

8. A special branch of the Department of Employment and Immigration should be established, and located in Canada Employment Centres, which would be invested with the power to investigate complaints and to make and enforce binding decisions.

9. The Immigration Settlement and Adaptation Program (I.S.A.P.) should make funds available to community organizations for the delivery of services to people on temporary employment authorizations. Funds should also be made available to assist domestic workers in lodging complaints of violations of the contract.

10. A list of these agencies should be supplied by the Immigration Department to all incoming domestic workers.

11. The Domestic Employment Branch, referred to in Recommendation Number Eight, should maintain a list of employers who have repeatedly violated the contract or who have not maintained suitable working conditions, and the Branch should refuse to confirm offers of employment for these employers.

12. A domestic worker should be able to change employers without jeopardizing her status in Canada.

13. A domestic worker should be able to use the services of Canada Employment Centres to find a new employer.

14. Given the significant number of temporary workers in Canada, the Government of Canada should sign the International Labour Conference's Convention #143 'concerning migrations in abusive conditions and the promotion of equality of opportunity and treatment of migrant workers.'

15. Establishment of legislation covering wages and working conditions of domestic workers on temporary employment authorizations should be immediately drafted and introduced into the House of Commons, in accordance with the policy of the Liberal Party in Opposition

and following the precedent established by the Caribbean and Mexican Seasonal Agricultural Workers' Program.

16. The Federal Government should bring pressure to bear on the Provincial Governments to ensure that these basic rights within the provincial jurisdiction are extended to all domestic workers.

17. Domestic workers who qualify under Unemployment Insurance Act and Regulations should be eligible to collect Unemployment Insurance benefits for sickness and maternity, and while seeking new employment.

18. Domestic workers leaving Canada should be provided with an Income Tax form and instructions for completion prior to leaving the country. The information regarding Income Tax and Canada Pension Plan reimbursement should be outlined in the initial letter given to the domestic worker upon arrival in Canada.

19. In recognition of the lack of affordable child care and the double workload carried by women in the paid labour force, the Income Tax Act should be amended to permit a person to claim a full deduction for the expense of employing a domestic worker. One of the mechanisms which the Federal Government should implement to ensure that domestic workers are paid the minimum wage is a provision in which the above tax deduction could be claimed only in situations where the minimum wage to the domestic worker has been paid.

Appendix 2 'Report and Recommendations for the Review of the Foreign Domestics Movement Program' submitted by The Toronto Organization for Domestic Workers' Rights (INTERCEDE) (December 1989)

Introduction

The Toronto Organization for Domestic Workers' Rights (INTERCEDE) presents this brief to Employment and Immigration Canada for the purpose of making recommendations for changes to the Foreign Domestic Movement (FDM) Program. INTERCEDE is a community-based non-profit organization founded in Toronto in 1979. It assists domestic workers and advocates for improvements in their employment conditions and immigration status. In 1989 alone, INTERCEDE has served an average of 327 clients, and has provided educational work in its monthly general meeting to an average of 430 domestic workers each month.

INTERCEDE believes that domestic workers and their organizations should be an integral part of the planned review of the FDM program as this program directly affects the lives of domestic workers and the general status of childcare and housework in Canadian society.

The recommendations in this report are based on the preliminary findings of a study INTERCEDE has recently (since October 1989) been conducting among domestic workers in Toronto with funding from the Ontario Women's Directorate. The study has so far involved participation of 359 foreign domestic workers in a survey and in-depth interviews with 15 domestic workers. The recommendations are also based on the feedback INTERCEDE has been receiving from its client foreign domestic workers about the legal and practical implications of the FDM Program since the program was initiated in 1981.

Based on the information INTERCEDE has collected from clients in the past eight years and the results of its recent research, INTERCEDE submits that the FDM, in its present legal form and its practical implications, has been discriminatory against immigrants who are predominantly visible minority women. It is also discriminatory against workers involved in domestic work, a type of work that has traditionally been accorded low status. In attempting to help solve the crisis of childcare and domestic work in Canadian society, this program has created new problems and new victims.

INTERCEDE considers the specific conditions of the FDM Program, which require foreign domestic workers to live-in the home of the employer for two years; restrict their movement to other employers and to other jobs; and places especially difficult requirements on domestic workers during their immigration assessments, are discriminatory in the sense that these onerous conditions apply to no other group of immigrant workers. It has been argued that domestic workers are in a privileged position compared to other groups of foreigners on temporary work permits. The consistently high and ever increasing demand in Canada for the services of domestic workers, however, does not justify the temporary worker status for this group of workers but rather supports an argument for permitting relaxed admission criteria for permanent status. Besides being discriminatory in relation to other immigrant workers, the restrictions that the FDM Program imposes on domestic workers have worsened the conditions of domestic workers and left them more vulnerable to abuse of their working conditions as well as to sexual abuse. These restrictions delay rather than enhance their adaptation to and full membership in Canadian society.

INTERCEDE proposes that the solution to the childcare crisis in Canada should not involve discriminatory measures that leave new immigrants exposed to a real possibility of enslavement and victimization. The solution must be formulated within the accepted principles of equality, justice and liberty that shape the Canadian political and judicial system.

Our remarks below are aimed at demonstrating the problems created by the requirements of the FDM program. With our recommendations that follow, we hope to contribute to a formulation of alternatives that will help eliminate gender and racial discrimination in Canadian society.

Results of Study and Recommendations: Living-In

Unpaid Overtime Work
The FDM Program requires foreign domestic workers with temporary employment authorization to live in the home of the employer during the first two years of their stay in Canada. This requirement which directly affects the private, personal as well as working lives of domestic workers does not apply to any other group of workers or immigrants in Canada. The information we have gathered during years of communication with our clients and our recent research among foreign domestic workers in Toronto has revealed that the live-in requirement leaves the domestic workers vulnerable to violations of her working rights as well as violations of her personal privacy and safety.

The survey conducted by INTERCEDE has demonstrated that there is a very strong correlation between living-in and working very long hours. According to our survey, only 24.2 per cent of live-in workers worked a standard work-week of 44 hours. 41.6 per cent worked an average of 45 to 50 hours a week. 19.9 per cent worked an average of 50 to 60 hours a week. And 6.8 per cent worked 60 or more hours. Often, there was either inadequate or no compensation for overtime work. Among the 359 respondents to our questionnaire, only 13 per cent of live-in domestic workers received the overtime rate of $7.50 an hour and 11.9 per cent were compensated by time off equal to 1.5 times every hour of overtime (these are the two legal forms of compensation for domestic workers according to the Ontario Employment Standards Act). 21.7 per cent were compensated with pay or time off less than what they were legally entitled to. And 39.3 per cent of live-in domestics received *no* compensation for overtime work. Among those who received no compensation for overtime work, 46.8 per cent reported working more than 50 hours a week. Even when the domestic worker is not asked to do extra 'active work,' her physical presence in the home of the employer in her 'off-hours' made it very likely that she would be asked to do simple 'favours' like watching the sleeping children or house-sitting because the employers are going out.

Although hours of work and compensation for overtime work are issues that do not directly concern the federal government and Employment and Immigration Canada, the strong connection between the live-in arrangement which the FDM program requires and a deterioration of conditions of work necessitates that Employment and Immigration looks into this matter.

Sexual Harassment
The live-in arrangement also leaves the domestic worker more vulnerable to sexual harassment. Although most Canadian employers are honest and trustworthy people, in the occasional cases where an individual employer is prone to sexually harassing female subordinates, the opportunity for abuse is greatly increased if there is a 'living-in' arrangement. During the interviews we recently conducted, 14 out of 15 domestic workers reported that they did not have locks for the doors to their rooms. This situation not only results in a lack of privacy but also causes serious discomfort and fear among some domestic workers. One domestic worker reported that she used to pile suitcases and furniture behind her door before sleeping at night so that she would be awakened if someone tried to enter. Where there is a living-in arrangement, quitting one's job because of sexual harassment (or any other type of abuse) is very difficult for domestic workers because it simultaneously means losing one's income and one's place to live.

Alienation/Isolation from Society
Another consequence of the live-in arrangement is that while it often makes the domestic worker uncomfortably close to the family of the employer, it isolates her from the rest of the society. As a workplace, the home is an isolating place for a domestic worker who toils alone. The isolation of the domestic worker becomes especially serious if the employer is one who does not respect the working hours of the employee. Since

overtime work without compensation is not at all unusual among live-in domestic workers, this abuse of the domestic worker's time conflicts with other requirements of the FDM for skill upgrading and social adaptation. Many of the domestic workers interviewed have expressed the difficulties of finding time to go for upgrading courses and be involved in community work when they are expected to work long hours as live-in workers.

Quality of Room and Board
The live-in requirement also creates problems of standardizing room and board. While domestic workers' wages are deducted a fixed sum for room and board, they have no choice over the quality of food or accommodation provided by their employers. During the interviews, several domestic workers expressed their dissatisfaction with inadequate amount of food provided. In these cases, they either remained underfed or had to spend extra money on food.

Based on the feedback it has received about the disadvantages created by the live-in requirement, INTERCEDE proposes that the live-in arrangement must be optional on the part of the domestic worker. Given the high costs of housing in the Metro Toronto area, many domestic workers would be likely to opt for this option. Our interviews, however, have revealed that even those domestic workers who would choose to live in would like to be given a choice on this matter.

Recommendation Number One

INTERCEDE urges the Ministry of Employment and Immigration to make 'living-in' an option for the domestic worker and *not* to *require* foreign domestic workers to live in the homes of the employers. As any free adult person in Canadian society, a domestic worker should be given the right to choose her place to live.

Recommendation Number Two

In cases where there is a live-in arrangement, INTERCEDE urges the Ministry of Employment and Immigration to lobby provincial government to treat the home of the employer as a regular workplace and to introduce measures to regulate and enforce working conditions – including health and safety and minimum employment standards – of domestic workers and their standards of room and board.

Freedom of Movement

Under the rules of the FDM Program, in the first two years of their stay in Canada, domestic workers are issued temporary work permits that restrict their employment to domestic work with a specific employer. Although domestic workers can change their employers with permission from Employment and Immigration, this requirement creates a system of indentured service in which the worker is essentially bonded to the employer. Going into an Immigration office and having to explain reasons for leaving a specific employer is often an intimidating experience for foreign domestic workers. The continued requirement to produce a release letter, makes it additionally difficult for the domestic worker especially if there is a bitter conflict with the employer, to move to a new employer.

Another obstacle to the freedom of movement of domestic workers is related to the requirement to produce a satisfactory employment record at the time of her immigration assessment for landed status. If a domestic has had two bad employers in a row, she is usually afraid that going to an Immigration office to ask for a third permit would jeopardize her chances of becoming a landed immigrant as she might be viewed as responsible for her bad employment situations. Such fear usually forces domestic workers to stay with a specific employer no matter how bad their working and living environment may be. Since there is no system in place in any of the provinces of Canada to determine whether employers are abiding by the terms of their contracts, the restrictions on the mobility of domestic workers imposed by the FDM places an unfair burden domestic workers who would like to change employers but fear (reasonably) that they will be treated as guilty of precipitating a bad employment relationship.

The above restrictions imposed by the FDM apply to no other group of immigrants who are free to select employers as they please. It is true that the situation of domestic workers is similar in some aspects to that of other foreigners who work with temporary work permits in Canada. While temporary work permits are issued to other groups of workers for whose areas of employment the demand is thought to be temporarily higher than supply, in domestic work, the demand has, since the late nineteenth century, been consistently higher than the supply of workers. This explanation used to justify the existence of temporary employment authorizations in other occupations, however, is totally inapplicable to the occupation of domestic work.

Recommendation Number Three

INTERCEDE urges Employment and Immigration Canada to stop the requirement of release letters as a condition for issuing new work permits.

Recommendation Number Four

INTERCEDE urges Employment and Immigration Canada not to restrict domestic workers in their choice of employer or term of employment. Domestic workers should be free as every other group of immigrants in Canada to be able to change their employers and not have to account to any government body as to the reasons why.

Recommendation Number Five

INTERCEDE urges Employment and Immigration Canada to stop issuing temporary employment authorizations to foreign domestic workers, but instead provide domestic workers with permanent residency status on landing.

Requirements for Landing
There are special criteria which are used in the evaluation of domestic workers for landing in Canada. Over and above the criteria that apply to other independent class immigrants, domestic workers are assessed on such criteria as upgrading, demonstating 'social adaptation' through performance of active involvement in and volunteer work in community organizations, and proving 'financial security' through their saving habits. These additional criteria do not apply to any other group of independent class immigrants whose occupations are in high demand in Canada. The expectation that foreign domestic workers should be able to do volunteer work during their very limited free time, and save out of their limited incomes suggests that domestic workers have to be rather extraordinary workers who might make 'super immigrants.'

Besides being very difficult to fulfill and requiring 'super human' qualities, the special assessment criteria also leave the impression among domestic workers that they need to prepare to work in other occupations rather than stay in domestic work to qualify for landing in Canada. In effect, therefore, the specific criteria applied to domestic workers serve to discourage those interested in pursuing long-term careers in domestic work and childcare from doing so!

Recommendation Number Six

INTERCEDE urges Employment and Immigration Canada to give higher points to domestic work in the occupational demand category during the assessment of domestic workers for landing. These points should correspond to the actual demand for domestic workers in Canada.

Recommendation Number Seven

INTERCEDE urges Employment and Immigration Canada to make available to domestic workers all the programs (such as language courses, skills upgrading courses, etc.) that are available to other immigrants.

Discrimination on the Basis of Gender and Marital Status
Another problem with the assessment criteria that apply to domestic workers is that, in their implementation, they work to discriminate against women who are married and/or women with dependents. This bias either discourages married women and women with dependent children from applying for the FDM or puts pressures on some applicants not to acknowledge marital status or list dependents. This situation is one that applies to no independent class *male* immigrants.

Recommendation Number Eight

INTERCEDE urges Employment and Immigration Canada to ensure that there is no discrimination against domestic workers with spouses or dependent children during their assessments for permanent landing.

Lack of Orientation and Information for Domestic Workers
Our interviews with Toronto domestic workers has revealed that they were given no orientation and little information, if any, on the FDM Program, about their employment contract and their conditions of work and rights prior to their arrival in Canada. Subsequent to their arrival, domestic workers have reported difficulties in obtaining information and clarifying issues. Given the conditions of their unique work environment that leaves domestic workers isolated, the lack of information

causes anxiety, and in many cases leaves domestic workers vulnerable to abuse of their working and personal rights.

Recommendation Number Nine

INTERCEDE urges Employment and Immigration Canada to institute a system of orientation which would inform foreign domestic workers, prior to their arrival in Canada, about the FDM (or the program that replaces it), about their contract, conditions of work, as well as about their human rights and employment rights in Canada, and community services specifically related to women.

Recommendation Number Ten

INTERCEDE urges Employment and Immigration Canada to continue providing information to domestic workers about their rights, over the phone if needed, after their arrival in Canada. It should be made clear, and addresses and telephone numbers be provided, to all incoming domestic workers that Immigration and Employment offices provide such information.

Recommendation Number Eleven

Where Employment and Immigration offices are unable to provide information and counseling to domestic workers, INTERCEDE urges Employment and Immigration Canada to fund non-profit community organizations in many localities which would do educative and advocacy work for domestic workers.

Notes

1 This chapter draws on work previously published in Daenzer (1993).
2 The 1981 policy change required domestic workers to work as non-landed immigrants for a period of two years. During this two-year indenture in domestic service, they could not change employers, and were prohibited from changing occupations.
3 See particularly Daenzer (1993, 125) in which a federal government bureaucrat is quoted on this issue.

4 PAC, RG 118, vol. 49, Immigration Policy Papers 1963, *Immigration from the Philippines*, April 1963, Report 3 legal pgs.
5 The point system, introduced in 1967, weighted immigrants' attributes on a point scale. Points were awarded for occupational training, education, official language fluency, and so on. Immigrants needed to have a minimum number of points (60 out of 100 at that time) to qualify for entry into Canada.
6 RG 76, vol. 83449, file 5850-6-4-533, part 2, Memorandum. To: Director, Region 'A.' From: Director, Foreign Branch. Re: Household Service Workers. Dated 29 November, 1968: '[T]he Regional Economists got together some time ago and simply agreed that the units of occupational demand for house-keepers and domestic service should be seven. I am not aware that they had before them any papers on which their judgement was based' (p. 1). At the time of the review by the Task Force, the Occupational Demand value had been reduced to zero.
7 RG 76, vol. 83449, file 5850-6-4-533, part 2, Department of Citizenship and Immigration, Memorandum. To: Regional Director 'A' Ottawa. From: Officer-in-Charge, Port of Spain. Subject. Household Service Workers. Dated 27 August 1968.
8 Memorandum to Mr. Axworthy. Addendum Step-by-Step Guidelines for Foreign Domestics. 'Domestics currently in Canada' B.(3)(c), p. 4.
9 For example: '[T]raining was to have occurred for a period of time sufficient to have provided the applicants with a developmental opportunity which will enable them to earn sufficient income to adequately maintain themselves.' In Policy Files series 8600-10. Memorandum from the Office of the Deputy Minister and Chairman. To: Hon. Mr. Axworthy. Re: Foreign Domestics. Stamped November 24, 1981. Noted as seen by the Minister, p. 1 of 13.
10 Department of Employment and Immigration, Policy Files 8600-10. Memorandum from the Office of the Deputy Minister and Chairman. To: The Minister, Hon. Mr. Axworthy. Re: Foreign Domestics. Stamped November 24, 1981. Noted as Seen By the Minister, p. 1 of 13 page document.

In addition, the arbitrariness of rewarding points for vocational preparation to domestic workers was to be discontinued. Some domestics were awarded 2 to 3 points for vocational preparation, and others were awarded zero points. Still, the suggestion to now award 10 points would be at the discretion of immigration officials and based upon an abstract assessment of the complexities of household service work.
11 Immigration Statistics: Employment and Immigration Canada. Ottawa. Run date: 21 April 1991.
12 Immigration Statistics; Employment and Immigration, Canada. Ottawa. Run date 22 April 1991.

13 Canada, Department of Employment and Immigration, Data on participation in the FDM program, Memorandum. To: Gene Hersak. From: Claude Langlois. Dated August 1, 1990. Unnumbered tables showing by year of entry.

14 According to the briefing document found in Policy File 8600-10 in a Memorandum to Hon. Mr. Lloyd Axworthy from the Deputy Minister and Chairman, regarding 'Foreign Domestics,' employers would be required to contribute $15 towards the skills development of their domestics and to grant them time off for night classes. In addition, employment counsellors would be required to pay attention to reported cases of abuses and attempt to find alternate employers for abused domestics. The entry of domestics as landed immigrants would still depend on the subjective assessment of overseas officials who regulated the acquisition of labour for Canada. The contribution would later be raised to $20.

15 Department of Employment and Immigration, Policy Files 8600-10, Memorandum. To: E. Donagher, Director General, Operations Branch. From: Director General, Policy and Program Development. Re: FDM – Policy Review. Dated June 4, 1985. See covering letter explaining rationale for review and revised policy.

16 Department of External Affairs, Memorandum. To: E. Donagher, Director General. Operations Branch. From: W.K. Bell, Director General, Policy and Programs Development. Attachment from: Visa Section, Canadian Embassy, Manila. Dated 18 February 1987. Paragraph 8, p. 3.

17 Canada, Employment and Immigration, Policy Files series 8600-10, Memorandum. To: Nicole Cullen, Director, Program Development, P & PD, Immigration. From: K.M. McIntosh, Director, Procedures and Instructions. Re: FDM Program: Draft Procedures. Dated January 28, 1987. 23 pp.

18 Canada, Employment and Immigration. Policy Files Series 8600-10. Operations Memorandum. 'Selection and Counselling of Foreign Domestics.' The Memorandum on Foreign Domestics which follows cancels and replaces existing instructions in Chapter IS 4.22 and IS 4.41. Dated 07.10.87. 25 pp. (including appendices).

19 Department of Employment and Immigration, Policy File 8600–10, ibid., Memorandum to Donagher, p. 14.

20 Departmental officials were aware of the non-legal status of the FDM. See for example: Department of External Affairs, copy in Policy Files 8600-10, letter. To: Mr. D.G.J. May, A/Chief, Admission Procedures Division, Operations Branch, Employment and Immigration. Signed by: C.M. Shaw, Director, Immigration and Refugee Affairs: 'The absence of a firm basis in law for the FDM is an issue which may prove problematic.'

21 Department of Employment and Immigration, Policy File 8600-10, Memorandum to Donagher, E. Director General, Operations Branch. From: Director General, Policy and Program Development. Re: FDM – Policy Review. Dated: June 4, 1985. 'Repeated Applications Abroad,' p. 11.
22 Department of Employment and Immigration, Statistical Review, Table 1. Foreign Domestic Movement Entrants to the Program by Region of Origin; 1982–1990. (Figures for 1990 were based on first 8 months only.)
23 Department of Employment and Immigration, Statistical Review, *Estimated Number of Persons Entering the Foreign Domestic Program by Country of Origin, All Countries Ever in Top Ten: 1988*. Also, *Estimated Number of Persons Entering the Foreign Domestic Program by Country of Origin, All Countries Ever in Top Ten: 1989*.
24 Government of Canada, 'Employment Authorizations Issued Abroad under the Foreign Domestic Movement and Live in Caregiver Program, principal applicants only and (extensions only),' run date: 30 April 1996.
25 Employment and Immigration, Canada, Letter. To: C.L. Rolenberg and S.R. Abraham. From: W.K. Bell, Director General, Recruitment and Selection Branch. Re: Name deleted for reasons of privacy. File: 3270-7-26400. Cross-filed in Policy File 8600-10, vol. 1. p. 1.

4

Little Victories and Big Defeats:
The Rise and Fall of Collective Bargaining
Rights for Domestic Workers in Ontario

JUDY FUDGE[1]

The working conditions of workers who are paid to perform domestic chores by the families in whose homes they live and work have proved to be remarkably resistant to legal regulation. The nature of this resilience is both ideological and material. While the logic of formal legal equality has accommodated demands by live-in domestic workers for the gradual extension of protective labour legislation to their work, this extension has been partial and ineffective. The ideologies of domesticity and privacy have historically combined to provide a justification for exempting these workers from some of the basic legal entitlements available to other workers. Moreover, even when these workers are entitled to some minimum labour standards, their isolation within private homes renders legal regulation ineffective. These workers continue to be 'squeezed between the public and private spheres, [belonging] to neither one or the other and [combining] the worst aspects of both' (Arat-Koc 1989, 41).

The recent history of the rise and fall of collective-bargaining rights for live-in domestic workers in Ontario provides an illuminating case study for understanding how these workers' location at the contradictory intersection of the public and private realms operates to their disadvantage. Compelled by the demands of domestic workers and their allies and committed to a social equity agenda, the New Democratic Party (NDP) government in Ontario legally recognized the right of domestic workers to bargain collectively. On 1 January 1993, fifty years after they were excluded from Ontario's first collective-bargaining legislation,[2] domestic workers were included in the Labour Relations Act,[3] which gave them the same collective-bargaining rights as the majority of workers in the province.[4] This was an important symbolic victory for the Toronto Organization for Domestic Workers Rights, INTERCEDE, which has represented domestic workers in Toronto since it was established in 1979. When the Conservative Party defeated the NDP government in June 1995, however, this victory was quickly reversed. On 7 November 1995, the exclusion of domestic workers from collective-bargaining rights was re-entrenched in the law.[5]

At one level, this case study demonstrates how quickly and casually legal victories for vulnerable workers can be defeated. At a deeper level, however, the legal treatment of domestic workers' collective-bargaining rights in Ontario demonstrates the extent to which formal legal recognition falls short of substantive equality. Together with women's groups, organizations that advocate on behalf of non-unionized workers, and the Ontario Federation of Labour, INTERCEDE made the treatment of domestic workers a test of the NDP government's commitment to social equity. But while these groups were able to persuade the government that the unequal treatment of domestic workers was no longer justified, formal equality did nothing to remedy the substantive inequality that marks a domestic worker's relationship with her employer. While in power, the NDP government acknowledged that the structure of domestic employment rendered the right to bargain collectively under the Labour Relations Act virtually meaningless for domestic workers.[6] Despite this, INTERCEDE and its allies sought to build upon the formal legal victory to press for measures to make the right to collective bargaining for domestic workers more than a legal formality. With the election of the Conservative Party, the struggle for effective legal entitlements for domestic workers has become even more difficult, for INTERCEDE and its members are now confronting a government that seems immune to demands of even formal or symbolic equality.

The tension between formal and substantive rights, and the relationship between ideology and material conditions, are themes shaping this chapter. This case study examines the rationales for the legal exclusion of domestic workers from collective bargaining legislation in Ontario in 1943, the political struggle and circumstances that led to their inclusion in 1993, and the political reversal that led to their exclusion, once again, in 1995. The first section focuses on the ideologies of domesticity and privacy – where domestic work, even when waged, is not regarded as constituting productive work, and where the personal nature of domestic labour renders it unsuitable for legal regulation. Moreover, since Canada has historically been an importer of live-in domestic workers, the 'servile' characterization of this work was reinforced by the racial and ethnic ideologies held by the majority of legislators, administrators, and citizens of a country that was formed as a white-settler colony. These ideologies converged with the economic and political subordination of domestic workers to freeze their unequal legal rights in the realm of work for fifty years (Leslie 1974, 71–3; Aitkin 1987).

The focus of the second section is the lobbying campaign for collective-bargaining rights for domestic workers conducted by INTERCEDE and allied groups. While these organizations were successful in challenging the ideological construction of domestic employment to obtain formal legal rights for domestic workers, the structural problem of the lack of fit between the collective bargaining scheme and domestic employment remained. What this meant was that, even though domestic workers were granted the same legal collective-bargaining rights as the majority of workers in the province, they were effectively denied access to collective bargaining because of the specific nature of their employment. This gap between formal and substantive collective-bargaining rights for domestic workers is explored in the third section. The fourth section suggests the kinds of institutional mechanisms that are necessary if domestic workers are ever to enjoy access to collective-bargaining. The fifth section examines both how easily the symbolic victory was reversed by the election of the Conservative government and the tenacity of ideologies that legitimate both the formal and substantive subordination of domestic workers. The chapter concludes by emphasizing the need for an ongoing political struggle for effective collective-bargaining rights for domestic workers, one which challenges both the ideological and material basis of their subordination.

Ideology and Inequality: The Exclusion of Domestic Workers from Employment Rights in Ontario

Domestic workers were the single largest category of paid female workers in Canada from 1871 to 1941. They were also the only category of female workers designated as 'desirable immigrants' by the Canadian government.[7] The 'desirability' of these women immigrants was, however, conditional, as it depended upon their chastity and ethnicity (Cunningham 1991, Chapter 2; Roberts 1988, 55–7; Valverde 1991, 124–8). Immigrants accounted for about one-third of the domestic workers in Canada until the outbreak of World War Two.[8] Of these female immigrants, British subjects were the preferred category until the 1940s. British female domestics were brought to Canada to redress the gender imbalance in western Canada and also to be the wives of prairie farmers. While, initially, racial distinctions were constructed using markers like nationality and language to exclude all but Anglo-Saxon immigrants, immigration policies changed and European women were recruited as servants. Racial distinctions became defined increasingly in terms of skin colour and European/non-European differences, such that race, understood in these terms, continued to operate as a bar in the vast majority of cases until the 1950s.[9]

Despite the fact that domestic workers were recruited to work and were paid wages, however low, their location within the family influenced how their relationship was categorized by law. Located in the home and associated with the realm of domesticity, domestic workers were, in some respects, attributed the status of a family member. For example, masters could receive a monetary award for damages against a man who seduced a female servant if they could prove that the female servant was previously of chaste character (Cunningham 1991, 65). The pregnancy of the servant was considered a loss for the master. This legal action, known as the tort of seduction, was also available to fathers and other male heads of households if their daughters or close female relatives were seduced. When it came to the master's duty to provide medical care and services for the servant, however, the relationship was characterized as one of contract and not one involving family status. Therefore, the master was not required to provide the necessities of life for the servant. Moreover, master and servant legislation, enacted in what was to become Canada during the 1830s and 1840s, treated the contractual relationship between masters and servants, including those employed to do domestic work, 'as a serious public matter, to the extent that contractual breaches were, under the legislation, criminal in nature' (Cunningham 1991, 82). But even while the contractual nature of the relationship was acknowledged in ways that did not benefit the domestic worker, the characterization of domestic workers as part of the family was the one that prevailed when they sought the protection of minimum-wage laws.

. The long hours and low wages of domestic workers prompted domestic workers to demand changes in their working conditions. As early as 1901, domestics across the country formed associations to overcome their isolation and engaged in collective action (Cunningham 1991, 127). They also lobbied for protective legislation that would provide them with a minimum wage and some regulation of their working conditions.

Domestic workers were not included in the provincial minimum-wage statutes enacted at the end of the 1910s.[10] Between 1913 and 1920 in Vancouver, Calgary, Winnipeg, Toronto, and Sydney, domestic workers' unions demanded the inclusion of domestic workers under the provincial minimum wages statutes and for the standardization of wages and hours (Cunningham 1991, 127–31; Epstein 1983, 222–37). In Ontario, this resistance provoked some results. The Farmer-Labour Alliance, which defeated the Conservatives to form the provincial government in 1920, drafted and introduced minimum-wage legislation that included domestic workers. This attracted the opposition of the Liberal Party, however, which attacked the legislation on the grounds that domestics and farm 'helpers' were in a position that differed from those of industrial workers. Since the former were provided their food and keep, they did not need assistance in dealing with their employers, H.H. Dewart, the Liberal leader, was reported to have claimed ('Bill to Protect Female Workers,' *The Mail and Empire*, 21 May 1920). To ensure the passage of the minimum-wage legislation, which was designed to improve the wages of women and children in the province, the Farmer-Labour Alliance dropped the provision concerning domestic workers. Ironically, this eliminated the largest single category of women workers from the legislation.

During the second half of the 1930s there was a resurgence of unionism generally, and among domestic workers' organizations in particular. A campaign in Ontario to bring domestic workers under minimum-wage legislation was initiated.[11] Responding to these pressures, the Ontario Ministry of Labour went so far as to draft an amendment to this effect. In 1937, however, the Minimum Wages Board recommended that it was 'inadvisable' to include domestic workers because of 'the difficulties of administration, the fact that most of such workers who are poorly paid receive board and room, and the apparent attitude of the general public in connection with government intervention in private homes' (Cunningham 1991, 141–2). The amendment was dropped and domestic workers continued to be excluded from employment-protection legislation. As we will see, the 'difficulties of administration' translates into the unwillingness of the state to intervene in private households. What have traditionally been seen as private and personal arrangements made by employers with their domestics is a recurring theme used to justify the exclusion of live-in domestic workers from basic employment legislation to this day.

When the legitimacy of collective bargaining was finally established in the wake of a wave of unionization and strike actions that swept through the manufacturing and resource sectors in the midst of the Second World War, collective-bargaining legislation was drafted and enacted in Ontario in 1943 (Willes 1979, 9–11). It was closely modelled on the Wagner Act, which had been implemented in the United States in 1937. Like its American counterpart, the Ontario statute excluded 'domestic servants.'[12] While the specific rationales offered for the exclusion are difficult to locate, the general reasons are not hard to discern. The Ontario legislation was designed to regulate the relations being established between unions and corporations in the manufacturing and resource sectors. It was not designed to facilitate collective bargaining for everyone (Fudge 1988, 283–345). Moreover, in the United States, the Senate report on the National Labor Relations Act noted that the exclusion of domestic workers was necessary for 'administrative reasons,' which was likely a short-hand for the difficulty of bringing collective bargaining into the privacy of the home.[13]

A supplementary rationale for the exclusion – one never explicitly mentioned in official reports – was the fact that the vast majority of domestic workers employed in private homes in the United States were black women. Racial segregation and exploitation was both an implicit rationale for, and a function of, the exclusion of domestic workers from the collective-bargaining legislation in the United States.[14] The absence of a history of a developed slave economy, plus racially restrictive immigration policies, resulted in a much smaller black population in Canada than in the United States. Thus, it is unlikely that a policy of racial segregation directly animated the exclusion of domestic workers from collective-bargaining legislation in Ontario and Canada. As the racial composition of the domestic workforce in Canada changed, however, the effect of the exclusion was much the same in Ontario as it was in the United States.

Despite a general decline in the demand for household labour after the Second World War, the demand for live-in domestics still exceeded the supply within the country. The servile nature of domestic work, which was characterized by a personalized, albeit subordinate, relationship between the domestic worker and her employer, combined with the poor pay and working conditions of such work to make it unattractive to Canadian citizens and residents who had other employment options, however limited.

The federal Immigration Department's racially restrictive immigration policies conflicted with the growing demand for live-in domestic workers as the labour market participation rate of women, and in particular married women, in Canada increased in the mid-1950s, and especially throughout the 1960s and 1970s. The racial and gender ideologies that had formerly been invoked to exclude Caribbean domestic workers were refashioned. These ideologies perpetuated the belief that black women had inherent attributes that suited them to particular jobs (Brand 1991, 14–15). In what began as a limited experiment in black immigration to meet a chronic labour shortage, the Caribbean Domestic Scheme was implemented.

Although recruited to Canada as domestic workers, many Caribbean women were not content with their lot as paid workers employed within private homes. The unequal immigration status of domestic workers under the employment visa program was a rallying point for domestic workers and the organizations that were formed to support them in their struggle for full immigration status (Epstein 1983, 228–9). In 1977, the plight of Caribbean domestic workers attracted widespread media attention when the Department of Immigration attempted to deport seven Jamaican women who had entered Canada under the former Caribbean Domestic Scheme. When these women, who had been residing in Canada for several years, applied in 1976 to sponsor their children as immigrants to Canada, the Department ordered them deported on the ground that they had violated the conditions of the Scheme by failing to list their dependent children on their applications to immigrate (Macklin 1994, 17–18; Calliste 1991, 108–9).

Under the rubric 'good enough to work, good enough to stay,' INTERCEDE, which was founded by a group of women researchers, academics, and lawyers in Toronto to end the international exploitation of domestic workers, coordinated a national campaign. The Toronto-based Jamaican mothers were supported by similar groups in Montreal, Ottawa, and Vancouver, to secure landed immigrant status for domestic workers coming to Canada (Epstein 1983, 231). After intensive lobbying, the immigration system was changed in 1980 so that domestic workers were given two-year temporary permits requiring them to live-in before they could apply for landed status. With this partial victory, INTERCEDE shifted focus and began to recruit domestic workers as active members. By 1984, INTERCEDE had received its first core funding from the federal government – the imprimatur of legitimacy.[15] Since then, it has received funding from both the federal and provincial governments. INTERCEDE has devoted a great deal of effort to obtaining policy and legal changes that will benefit domestic workers, as well as providing advice, workshops, and social events for its members. A centrepiece of its work is the recognition of the value of domestic workers' work. In addition to demanding that the federal government abolish the temporary work authorization program and substitute full landed immigrant status for immigrant domestic workers, it called upon the Ontario government to include domestic workers under all employment-related legislation.

Prior to INTERCEDE's pressure that the Employment Standards Act be extended to include domestic workers, these workers were excluded from all of the basic labour standards. As a result of pressure from INTERCEDE and other groups, at the beginning of 1981, the Conservative government amended the legislation to provide minimum daily, weekly, and monthly wages to be paid to live-in domestic workers (Townson 1987, 3). They continued to be excluded, however, from the sections of the Act dealing with maximum hours of work and overtime pay. The combined effect of this exclusion and the provision of minimum daily, weekly, and monthly wages was that domestic workers could be required by their employers to work more than eight hours per day, thereby bringing their actual hourly wage below the minimum rate (Townson 1987, 3). The minister of labour at that time, Robert Elgie, rejected INTERCEDE's demands that live-in domestic workers be guaranteed the minimum provincial hourly wage. In justifying this unequal treatment of live-in domestic workers, Elgie stated: 'We did not want to reduce the market for domestic workers by imposing too high a minimum and requiring a lot of bookkeeping by families' (Townson 1987, 38). According to him, domestic workers could simply find alternative employment if they were dissatisfied with their wages. But what he failed to mention was that the temporary work authorization permits seriously limited, if not totally eliminated, the labour mobility of domestic workers. Combined with the de facto indentured status of live-in domestic workers, the government's concern that maximum hours of work and overtime provisions would impose an onerous burden on private households ensured that employers had a cheap source of domestic labour.

INTERCEDE continued to agitate for overtime protections for domestic workers. The Liberal government elected in 1985 also opposed these changes, claiming that the potential increase in the cost of employing live-in domestic workers would 'upset the childcare arrangements of parents some of whom may already be in a financial squeeze' (Arat-Koc 1989, 48 quoting from Fruman 1987, C-1). In 1987, after INTERCEDE launched a challenge to the exemption of live-in domestic workers from maximum hours of work and overtime provisions as a violation of the equality rights guaranteed under the Canadian Charter of Rights and Freedoms, the Liberal government responded.[16]

The result of INTERCEDE's endeavours was Regulation 322, which provides specific minimum employment standards for domestic workers. Domestic workers continue to be excluded from the maximum hours of work protection, which is 48 hours per week. Where the domestic worker is required by her employer to work in excess of 44 hours in a week, the excess work time may be granted as time off (lieu time) or pay, both at a rate of 1.5 hours for each excess hour worked.[17] The net effect of these regulatory changes is still to treat domestic workers unequally as compared with other workers (domestic workers are only legally entitled to compensatory time rather than overtime pay and have no limit on the number of hours they can be required to work), but not as badly as they were treated before.

Despite these legal changes, overwork and undercompensation continue to be rated as the most serious employment problems experienced by domestic workers. A 1989 study of the working conditions of domestic workers in Toronto conducted by INTERCEDE showed that an alarming number of domestic workers were denied their basic employment rights (Arat-Koc and Villasin 1990, 5–7). Sixty-five per cent of the 576 live-in domestic workers surveyed by INTERCEDE reported that they were regularly required to work overtime. Only 33 per cent of live-in domestic workers who routinely performed overtime work received the legal compensation of time-and-a-half pay or lieu time; 43.7 per cent received no compensation whatsoever.

The problem of unequal standards for domestic workers, however, goes beyond the minimal legal standards; even these standards are not effectively enforced. Enforcement of the minimum standards is dependent upon the domestic worker filing a complaint with the Employment Standards Branch of the Ministry of Labour. This individualized complaints mechanism is simply not effective for enforcing domestic workers' employment rights. Many domestic workers lack knowledge of their basic legal entitlements. Moreover, the risk of jeopardizing their jobs and more importantly, their chances of becoming landed immigrants, renders many domestic workers afraid of making a formal complaint.[18]

Violations of basic employment standards are common and the claims submitted to the Employment Standards Branch represent only the tip of the iceberg. Because of the live-in requirement under the immigration policy regime, job loss carries more drastic consequences for domestic workers than for any other category of worker. When a domestic worker loses her job as a result of a complaint, she loses the roof over her head. An INTERCEDE study found that it was not uncommon for domestic workers to be fired without notice; in fact, 'several recounted experiences of being thrown out on the street, some at night and in the middle of winter' (Serwonka 1991, 6).

This has led INTERCEDE to the conclusion that the most significant problem facing domestic workers is effective enforcement of employment standards, and that this is possible only through unionization or other forms of collective representation. The exclusion of domestic workers from collective-bargaining legislation was just the most obvious manifestation of the problem. The challenge INTERCEDE faced was to develop mechanisms for representing domestic workers in their dealings with their employers and to ensure that the government would implement such mechanisms.

Formal Equality: A Symbolic Victory

The election of the New Democratic Party as the government of Ontario in 1990 was auspicious for INTERCEDE. The NDP had explicitly campaigned on a social equity agenda and it had promised to reform labour relations law in order to bring it up to date for the 1990s. In its throne speech, the government reiterated its commitment. When in opposition, the NDP had also often acted as INTERCEDE's ally. For example, members of the NDP provincial caucus had supported INTERCEDE's legal challenge to the unequal protections provided under the Employment Standards Act.[19] Thus, INTERCEDE thought there was a chance to achieve collective bargaining for domestic workers.

Bob Mackenzie, then minister of labour, kicked off the labour law reform process in March 1991 by appointing an external committee to review the Labour Relations Act. It was composed of representatives of business and labour, the majority of whom were lawyers, and chaired by Kevin Burkett, an experienced arbitrator and former member of the Ontario Labour Relations Board. Predictably, the business and labour representatives split over the very premise of the need to reform the legislation in order to make it easier to organize workplaces in Ontario and issued separate reports. While the business representatives did not mention the exclusion of domestic workers in their report, in their separate report the labour representatives urged the government to include domestic workers under the collective-bargaining law.

The labour report recommended the immediate inclusion of domestic workers on the ground that the continuing exclusion of these workers under the Labour Relations Act violated the guarantee of equality rights in the Canadian Charter of Rights and Freedoms. The labour representatives went on to note that, while the 'removal of the exclusion would mark a significant step in ensuring equal access to rights' contained in the collective-bargaining act, 'the problems facing domestics ... must be addressed by other sectoral initiatives' (Ontario Ministry of Labour, 14 April 1991, 16–17). In effect, they acknowledged that simply including domestic workers under collective-bargaining law would not necessarily result in any improvements in domestic workers' employment conditions unless the legislation was further modified to address the specific problems that domestic workers confronted.

In November, the Ministry of Labour released a discussion paper on the proposed reform of the Ontario Labour Relations Act (Ontario Ministry of Labour 1991). Emphasizing the themes of equity and partnership, the discussion paper identified the changing nature of work, the workplace and the workforce. It argued further that in order to facilitate collective-bargaining for many workers effectively denied access to bargaining under the Act, the legislation had to be reformed. In addition to listing a number of preferred changes and canvassing a number of possible solutions, the discussion paper invited submissions to public consultations that would be held throughout the province. It also promised another consultation when the draft bill was before the legislative committee.

Domestic workers received some attention in the discussion paper, which stated that,

> these employees are overwhelmingly women; they are frequently immigrants or employed on work permits; and they often work in isolated or particularly vulnerable situations. Domestic employment is characterized by low pay and in many cases inferior benefits. Only two other provinces exclude domestics from collectively bargaining. (Ontario Ministry of Labour 1991 13–14).

It concluded that the retention of the existing exclusion could not be justified. It did, however, acknowledge the limitations in simply including them:

The government recognizes that because domestics often work alone or in very small groups, the removal of the existing exclusion of these employees may not result in effective access to collective-bargaining arrangements. Where employees work alone, they are not eligible to organize and bargain because, under the Act, there must be more than one employee for collective-bargaining to be viable. (Ontario Ministry of Labour 1991, 14)

Consequently, the government announced its intention to give future consideration to additional means of enhancing domestic workers' access to collective bargaining.

INTERCEDE joined with a number of groups, such as Parkdale Community Legal Services Inc., the National Action Committee on the Status of Women, the Ontario Coalition for Better Child Care, the Ontario Women's Action Committee, the Workers' Information and Action Centre, and the Coalition for Fair Wages and Working Conditions for Homeworkers, which wanted to ensure that the labour legislation was reformed to provide real access to collective-bargaining for women and other people located at the bottom of the labour market. Together, these groups formed a coalition called Women for Labour Law Reform. The coalition held a one-day workshop on 11 January 1991 in Toronto attended by about 90 participants, many of whom were domestic workers, on the impact of the reforms on women workers. The treatment of domestic workers was seen by the participants as a prime example of the distinction between symbolic reform and substantial benefit. The coalition was concerned to develop proposals that made a real difference for women workers. It continued to act as a clearing house for information, and as a pressure group on the government throughout the reform process.[20]

INTERCEDE submitted a brief to the minister of labour that emphasized the employment situation of domestic workers and the inadequacies of the collective-bargaining model in relation to it. The government's promise to get rid of the exclusion was welcome. The brief raised the concern, however, that unless additional measures of enhancing domestic workers' access to organization and collective bargaining were developed and implemented, simply including domestic workers under the Labour Relations Act was only a token right. It recommended a series of reforms designed to lead to collective bargaining by domestic workers; the key proposal was the formation of a central registry of domestic workers (INTERCEDE 1992). A number of other organizations also urged the government to implement additional measures for domestic workers.[21]

Business groups took a general no-holds-barred approach in their opposition to the labour-law reform proposals.[22] Specific objections to the proposal to delete the exclusion of domestic workers were not widespread, however, although they did exist. The Board of Trade of Metropolitan Toronto urged the government to retain the unequal treatment of domestic workers on the ground that the rationales for their exclusion were still viable. In language reminiscent of that uttered over half a century earlier, the board of trade stated that

> the employer/employee relationship in the domestic situation is, and always will be, a unique one. It is one in which the employer takes an individual into his/her home to assist in household duties, and, more importantly, to care for other family members. It is therefore a very personal relationship and, at both the hiring and termination stages, is extremely subjective. While the employee (the domestic) may be a very responsible, competent individual, one can legitimately conclude in a specific family environment that a certain individual may not be suitable. To bring domestics under the Act, with the consequent right to collectively bargain, would therefore seriously affect this personal/subjective relationship, and would derogate from the employer's right to decide what is best in his/her family environment. Neither the government, nor a union should be able to intervene in these private functions of a household as a fundamental matter of public policy. (Board of Trade of Metropolitan Toronto 1991, 3)

In addition to the 'subjective and personal nature of the employment relationship,' the board of trade pointed out that the '"structure" of the domestic workforce renders the concept of including domestics under the Act unworkable' (1991, 3). According to the board, the geographic dispersal of domestic workers in individual homes would make it hard, if not impossible, to establish a viable bargaining unit under existing labour law. It also vetoed, however, the idea of the hiring hall, once again citing the personal and subjective relationship between a domestic worker and her employer.

A confidential document prepared for the Cabinet analysing a range of policy options available to the government and their likely political consequences was leaked in the summer of 1991 (Ontario 1991). Among the options identified, two were important: the repeal of the domestic exclusion in the labour relations statute; and the government's intention to study the extension of collective bargaining to domestic workers in the wider context of a study of broader-based or sectoral bargaining

(Ontario 1991, 10–11). On the positive side, the document noted that this would allow domestics to organize and extend the option of collective bargaining to a group of workers especially in need of protection. Such an initiative would be widely supported by women's organizations, immigrant groups, and other advocates of the disadvantaged. The necessity of some form of broader-based or sectoral bargaining to give domestic workers effective bargaining strength was also emphasized (Ontario 1991, 10–11). On the negative side, however, it was noted that objections might be raised to the prospect that a person's home could become a unionized workplace.

The leak of the Cabinet document provoked a tirade of business opposition.[23] The government was careful to assuage the fears of the business community by distancing the final legislative package from the reform options presented to Cabinet and stressing the remaining round of public consultations. Bill 40, the draft legislation, was released in June 1992 alongside a package of highlights outlining the original proposals, the impact of consultation, and the government's changes. The bill repealed the exclusion of domestic workers; but it did nothing else for them. The information package noted that there was little opposition to removing the exclusion, although a number of organizations said that this change would do little to address the needs of domestic workers and that it should be supplemented with other measures.[24] INTERCEDE and its allies continued to press the government to commit itself to implementing some sort of mechanism that would promote collective-bargaining for domestic workers. In the end, the legislation was amended to repeal the exemption, and, in the absence of almost any publicity, the government announced that it would establish a task force to examine the possibility of extending broader-based bargaining in Ontario.

The Structural Problem

The removal of the exclusion of domestic workers from collective-bargaining legislation signalled the erosion of an explicit reliance on the ideology of privacy to deny domestic workers formal equal rights with other workers. Moreover, legal recognition of the right of domestic workers to bargain collectively was an acknowledgment of the value of their labour. The board of trade's submission did not arouse much sympathy from the government and the exclusion smacked of naked inequality.

But simply getting rid of the exclusion was not much of a step forward. As everyone who participated in the reform process acknowledged, the absence of additional changes would mean that very few domestic workers would be able to enjoy collective bargaining. By itself, the symbolic change was simply that – symbolic. Domestic workers, their organizations, and their allies would still need to persuade the government to introduce measures to make collective bargaining a reality.

The problem with simply repealing the section excluding domestic workers was that there were barriers in the collective-bargaining legislation and its administration by the Ontario Labour Relations Board that made it virtually impossible to organize domestic workers for collective bargaining. Where employees work alone, they are not eligible to organize and bargain because, under the Labour Relations Act, there must be more than one employee for a bargaining unit to be certified and for collective bargaining to be legally enforced.[25] Since most domestic workers work alone, this is enough to deny them access to collective bargaining.

Even if the government had amended the Labour Relations Act to allow the Labour Relations Board to certify single-employee bargaining units, this would likely not have resulted in effective access to collective bargaining for domestic workers. Single-employee units offer very few of the benefits of unionization for the workers themselves, and for the labour movement in general. Not only is it prohibitively expensive for unions to organize and administer single-employee units, such small units simply do not have the bargaining power to secure significant improvements in the terms and conditions of employment. This is particularly true for domestic workers. Collective-bargaining law in Canada is premised on the belief that it is best to let the parties work out the terms and conditions of collective agreements. In the event of an impasse, and after negotiations, mediation, and conciliation procedures have been exhausted, the parties are entitled to have recourse to economic sanctions (the strike and lock-out) to reach an agreement. Since foreign domestic workers are required to reside at their place of employment,[26] it would be virtually impossible for them to engage in effective strike action without risking loss of their residence. Given that employers are entitled to lockout employees to back up their demands, domestic workers could well lose their residence in the event of a collective-bargaining dispute.

Basic structural elements in Ontario's collective-bargaining law, including an emphasis on single-employer units and the resort to economic sanctions to resolve bargaining impasses, are at odds with key features of the employment situations of domestic workers. For these reasons, abolishing the exclusion of domestic workers from the Labour Relations Act did not result in concrete improvements in the working conditions of domestic workers.

Giving Substance to Collective Bargaining

It was clear to INTERCEDE that some form of collective representation of domestic workers was necessary to enforce their employment rights. The problem was in identifying what form this representation should take and compelling or persuading employers to recognize it. Assuring the NDP government's commitment to enforcement of such representation was also problematic. Simple legal recognition of the right to bargain collectively without additional measures to facilitate its exercise had not resulted in collective bargaining in those provinces in which domestic workers were included under labour-relations legislation. In seven out of ten provinces, domestic workers have been formally included under collective-bargaining legislation.[27] Despite this, domestic workers' unions and associations across the country have not been able to use the law to achieve effective collective-bargaining. This is because the collective-bargaining legislation in these jurisdictions shares with Ontario the central notion that collective bargaining is to take place at the level of the individual workplace. As Lorina Serafico of the Committee for Domestic Workers' and Caregivers' Rights in Vancouver, explained, domestic workers are not able to organize collectively without some form of legislation that broadens collective bargaining beyond the individual employer's home. To bring equal rights to domestic workers, she stated that there must be sectoral bargaining and a central registry of employers, regulated and supervised by a tripartite committee (Fairey 1993, 9–11).

The hurdle INTERCEDE faced was how to organize and represent domestic workers dispersed throughout the City of Toronto and the rest of the province, in employers' homes. Some degree of central organization to coordinate domestic workers collectively was needed to overcome their physical isolation. Workplace unionism, however, would remain ineffective as long as the workplace was defined as the individual household. Domestic workers bargaining on such an individualized basis could not have much economic clout. The other existing option, craft unionism, was and is simply not viable for domestic workers. Craft unionism depends upon the union exercising a monopoly over employees with certain skills or over the labour force in a particular occupation. To be successful, craft unions must exercise sufficient bargaining clout to force employers to hire only through a hiring hall, which the union runs. To prevent disruptions due to strikes, employers have an incentive to hire only union labour and to bargain exclusively with the union. Construction work is one of the few remaining examples of craft unionism. Hiring halls and craft unionism, however, are not an option for INTERCEDE so long as foreign domestic workers are required under the federal government's immigration policy to live in their employers' homes. Domestic workers are effectively denied the strike weapon; to exercise it means they lose both their residence and their landed status.[28]

What INTERCEDE decided it needed was a legislated variation of a hiring hall (Epstein 1983, 235), but one that does not depend on strikes to ensure employer recognition. Thus, INTERCEDE's first step was to call for the establishment of a central registry. Employers would be required to register if they employed domestic workers, and the workers could do so if they chose (INTERCEDE 1992). Employment agencies that placed domestic workers would also be required to register. Mandatory registration of employers was considered necessary to make domestic work visible and employers accountable for minimum employment standards. Concerns for the privacy of individual employers of domestic workers were dismissed on two grounds. First, as a condition for obtaining a live-in migrant domestic worker, employers are required to register with the Department of Immigration. Second, the fact that householders are prepared to turn their private homes into workplaces by employing a domestic worker compromises their claim to privacy. Since enforcement by individual domestic workers of their employment rights leaves them too vulnerable to retaliation by employers in whose homes they work and live, INTERCEDE proposed that the central registry should be authorized to prosecute a complaint on a domestic worker's behalf.

INTERCEDE has strong contacts with domestic workers throughout Toronto, and there are a number of agencies that have ongoing dealings with them. Despite these formal linkages, however, information about advocacy organizations among domestic workers depends mainly upon word of mouth – informal communication. A central registry, however administered, would provide a mechanism for contacting domestic workers, informing them of their rights, and representing them in disputes with employers. To ensure that it would be effective, sanctions for failing to register or adhere to standards would have to be provided. The agency administering the registry would have to be given enough clout to enforce such sanctions.

Apart from the registry, a number of crucial questions that require close consideration remained to be resolved. Should the agency administering the registry take the form of a union; if so, how would it be structured? Should it be a quasi-governmental agency or a tripartite committee composed of representatives of domestic workers, their employers, and the government? Or perhaps a workers' cooperative would be better, as it would take over the business of sending domestic workers to employers, thereby squeezing out the private employment agencies that act as gatekeepers to domestic work.[29] If employment agencies were to continue to operate, what role should they play and how should they be regulated? Should employers be required to organize and be bound by the decisions of an organization that represents them? Was this feasible? Was it possible to move from a mechanism designed to enforce minimum standards to a form of broader-based bargaining where representatives of domestic workers negotiated the general terms of the employment relationship with representatives of employers? If so, how?

INTERCEDE was not alone in seeking more effective means to organize workers employed in private homes. The International Ladies Garment Workers Union (ILGWU), together with the Coalition for Justice for Homeworkers, was organizing homeworkers in the Toronto garment industry over the same period.[30] These organizations joined forces to address the issue of broader-based bargaining. During the labour-law reform debate, broader-based bargaining had been identified as crucial if the most disadvantaged workers in Ontario, many of whom are women and immigrants, were to be collectively represented.[31]

There are significant differences between the employment situations of domestic workers and homeworkers in the garment industry. The former work out of the employer's home, for example, and the latter are engaged in a system of production for profit (Ontario District Council 1993). But there are also some salient similarities. Their situations are characterized by isolation and vulnerability; traditional forms of representation and collective-bargaining do not work; and as women, often women of colour, they are at the bottom of the labour market. Thus, INTERCEDE and the ILGWU applied for and received funding from the Ontario Women's Directorate to undertake a joint study of possible forms of broader-based bargaining in their sectors. Their report, which identifies some models for a central registry and broader-based bargaining for domestic workers,[32] was distributed widely throughout the labour movement as a means of educating unionized workers about the need for broader-based collective bargaining.

This report goes some way towards answering some of the questions about the most effective and democratic form of representation for domestic workers. INTERCEDE, however, still faced the huge task of trying to implement its proposals. Employers and employment agencies would be sure to resist any major shake-up which would increase the power of domestic workers. INTERCEDE would need an ally in the provincial government if collective bargaining was ever to become a reality.

Re-entrenching Inequality

The NDP government's repeal of the exclusion of domestic workers from the labour relations legislation did not, in sum, enable them to bargain collectively. It did, however, signal a successful challenge to the ideologies of privacy and the sanctity of the family. These ideologies had permitted employers to hide the employment relationship with their domestic workers within the privacy of their homes. In this sense it was a victory. Moreover, its social democratic commitment to an equity agenda, which explicitly addressed the disadvantaged situation of women workers of colour located at the bottom of the labour market, went some way towards challenging the racial subordination of domestic workers. This symbolic victory, although it did not result in the improvement of working conditions for live-in domestic workers or provide them with effective collective-bargaining structures, was not hollow. Rather, it indicated the government's initial willingness to challenge prevailing orthodoxies that operated to the disadvantage of domestic workers. But the NDP government's support for providing domestic workers with effective collective-bargaining rights dissipated as it faced continuing opposition to its policies. Thus, it failed to make good on its promise to appoint a task force to consider broader-based bargaining structures for vulnerable workers.

The political tide and economic conditions that led to the election of the NDP on a social equity platform in the fall of 1990 turned during the second half of the government's mandate. Declining wages, increasing unemployment, tax hikes, and an expanding government deficit proved to be fertile ground in which right-wing populist parties could grow by exploiting the fears of the beleaguered middle class. Moreover, business opposition to general labour-law reform introduced by the NDP govern-ment was vitriolic and unabating (Jain and Muthuchidambaram 1995). The continuing deep recession in Ontario and the media-fed preoccupa-tion with the deficit prompted the NDP government to legislate what were in effect wage reductions in the public sector and to reduce public sector employment, in the form of the Social Contract, in 1993.[33] This caused serious divisions in the labour movement. Moreover, the deep-ening recession fuelled a backlash against the NDP's equity agenda, which the Conservative Party both cultivated and exploited during the spring 1995 election. With its traditional support split and many party activists alienated by the Social Contract, the NDP government was soundly defeated at the polls.

The Conservative Party was elected on a platform called the 'Com-mon Sense Revolution' that targeted the public sector and the most dis-advantaged of Ontario's population as the cause of the province's economic woes. The Conservative government took the reigns of power by announcing that it was open for business. Its first initiatives were drastically to reduce provincial welfare rates by 21.6 per cent and to announce huge lay-offs in the public sector and extensive government spending cuts. As a second step, the Conservative government reversed the NDP's labour policies. The Employment Equity Act was abolished, as was the Agriculture Labour Relations Act, and the NDP's amend-ments to the Labour Relations Act were revoked with a minimum of public consultation.

Elizabeth Witmer, the new Conservative minister of labour, intro-duced the government's amendments to the Ontario Labour Relations Act on 4 October 1995. Characterizing the NDP changes as 'a barrier to jobs, growth, and investment,' Witmer announced that her new labour relations legislation (Bill 7) would 'restore the balance in labour rela-tions, spur economic growth, and generate new job opportunities for workers.'[34] In addition to the general repeal of the NDP amendments, Witmer announced that she was introducing a series of provisions that would promote workplace democracy. The thrust of these provisions was to target trade unions as impediments to democracy by requiring secret votes as a prerequisite for the formation of trade unions, the ratifi-cation of collective agreements, and the authorization of strikes. The new legislation also made it easier for employees to decertify trade unions once they had achieved collective-bargaining rights.[35]

As part of the repeal of the NDP amendments, the exclusion of domestic workers from the Labour Relations Act was re-established. No specific rationale for this decision was offered by either the minister or her government. In its brief to the minister of labour, the Ontario Federation of Labour (OFL) underscored the government's dissemblance in revoking the right of domestic workers to bargain collectively while simultaneously avowing a commitment to workplace democracy. Commenting on the Conservative government's reversal of the NDP's legislative policy of broadening access to the right to collective bargaining to employees previously deprived of that right, the OFL stated that

> some of the most marginal and vulnerable sectors of society, domestics and agricultural workers were given the right to collectively bargain for the first time. These changes were consistent with labour legislation in most other provinces in Canada. It is difficult to understand why a government which has professed concern for enhanced democracy in the workplace would entirely remove the right to organize from these members of the Ontario work force. The legislative repeal of such protection raises serious questions as to whether the equality and associational rights of these employees has been infringed, and will as a result lead to court challenges on constitutional grounds.[36]

Complaints that the exclusion of domestic workers violated the commitment to formal legal equality did not move the Conservative government. On 7 November 1996, the government's labour law changes were passed into law.

The May 1996 budget of the Ontario government announced a $7.5 million capital grants fund for nine Ontario daycare centres. This was the product of considerable lobbying from daycare advocates, however, responding to a dramatic cut in support for provincial daycare subsidies. Moreover, according to Kerry McQuaig of the Ontario Coalition for Better Child Care, funding was provided only for nine of twenty-five centres faced with closure. Between October 1995 and May 1996, thirty-five daycare centres in Ontario had already closed, and twenty-seven new daycare centres in school buildings had failed to open due to lack of funding (Toughill 1996).

Families must now demonstrate greater 'self-reliance' in making child-care arrangements. For those unfortunate enough not to have family support to take care of children while parents work, they will have to rely on an increasingly deregulated private child-care network. Moreover, the federal government has failed to come through on its promise to establish a national child-care program.

With publicly funded support for child care declining, it is likely that an increasing number of dual-income-earning and single-parent families will have to rely on live-in domestic workers recruited from outside the country for child care. Of course, the availability of this form of child care depends upon the economic circumstances of the families who are forced to rely on private arrangements. By abolishing the right of live-in domestic workers to rely on the Labour Relations Act to assist them in unionizing and collective-bargaining, the Conservative government is effectively subsidizing the costs to families who resort to live-in domestic workers to meet their child care needs by ensuring that these workers remain overworked and underpaid. Moreover, Labour Minister Witmer has announced that the Employment Standards Act will be overhauled. This does not bode well for domestic workers, since the minister accompanied her announcement with the statement that legislation should continue to protect workers in Ontario, while at the same time encouraging the workplace parties to assume greater responsibility for self-reliance (Mittelstaedt 1996). It is precisely the fact that domestic workers are isolated within the privacy of their employers' homes that has exacerbated their vulnerability to exploitation.

Conclusion

The NDP's inclusion of domestic workers under the Labour Relations Act extended legal recognition of the right to unionize and bargain collectively to a group of workers that had been excluded for fifty years. It symbolized a challenge to the deeply rooted and pervasive ideological construction of paid domestic labour as a private matter that should be protected from state intervention and forms of collective representation. Although the NDP failed to address the material circumstances of live-in domestic workers that undermined their ability to enjoy these legal rights, the extension of formal, legal equality functioned as a symbolic stepping stone both to the recognition of the value of domestic work provided by immigrant women and to their effective organization and representation in employment-related matters.

But this symbolic victory proved to be extremely vulnerable to the concatenation of ideological, political, and economic forces that swept the Conservative Party to power in 1995. The Conservative government's ideology of self-reliance, its antipathy to government regulation and trade unions, and its opposition to equity claims by members of racial minorities fuelled its decision to exclude domestic workers from the collective-bargaining rights available to most other workers in the province. Moreover, it is extremely unlikely that this government will respond to lobbying efforts that invoke the logic of equal rights for workers who have been historically disadvantaged by the devaluation of domestic labour, the sanctity of the private household, and racial subordination. Thus, it may be necessary for INTERCEDE and the domestic workers it represents to once again invoke the equality rights guaranteed in the Charter of Rights and Freedoms to raise the political profile of the enduring unequal legal treatment of domestic workers.

Collective representation of domestic workers is a long-term goal with many stages and skirmishes along the way. Any positive legal reform will ultimately depend upon the political pressure that INTERCEDE can generate. Alone against their employers, foreign domestic workers have no effective bargaining clout. Under current laws, INTERCEDE has no right to compel employers to recognize it as the representative of the domestic workers. Legal recognition of a collective organization of domestic workers would require new and different laws, whose very implementation would mark both a change in the balance of political forces and the reconception of the value of domestic labour provided by immigrant women workers. It is a difficult time to call for creative and effective forms of employment regulation. Moreover, INTERCEDE's own experience has shown that, for legislation to be effective, there needs to be a collective organization to ensure that it is enforced.

For domestic workers, their employment situation is made more vulnerable by the immigration regime which governs them.[37] Thus, INTERCEDE and other such organizations have expended a great deal of time and effort lobbying the federal government for changes to the immigration program for domestic workers. Like many advocacy organizations for people in the most vulnerable positions in society, it is underfunded and overworked. But despite these difficulties, INTERCEDE has provided a collective voice for domestic workers in the Toronto area specifically, and for all domestic workers' concerns more generally across the country. It has forced repeated governments, gradually and grudgingly, at both the provincial and federal levels, to grant domestic workers employment-related rights. INTERCEDE recognizes that collective organization and representation are absolutely necessary to limit the exploitation of domestic workers and it has linked its struggle to those of other groups which understand that collective representation is necessary for real equality. Moreover, despite the odds, domestic workers in Canada have continually organized to overcome their isolation. INTER-CEDE draws upon this legacy in its struggle to develop durable and democratic collective organizations of domestic workers that wield enough power to challenge their subordination and to change their living and working conditions.

Notes

1 I would like to thank Felicita O. Villasin for her gracious help in providing me with information for this chapter. All errors are my own.
2 The Collective Bargaining Act, S.O. 1943, c. 4, s. 24(b).
3 Labour Relations Act Amendments, S.O. 1992, c. 21.
4 In addition to domestic workers, other workers, defined either in terms of professional status or sector, were historically excluded. Firefighters and police officers, for example, do not bargain under the Labour Relations Act but under specific statutes. Agricultural workers were excluded at the same time as domestic workers. The NDP government, however, had enacted specific legislation granting the former modified collective-bargaining rights; see The Agricultural Labour Relations Act, 1994 (Bill 91), which received Royal Assent on 23 June 1994. This Act was later repealed by the Conservative government at the same time domestic workers were once again excluded from the collective-bargaining legislation.
5 An Act to restore balance and stability in labour relations and to promote economic prosperity and to make consequential changes to statutes concerning labour relations, S.O. 1995, c. 1, Schedule A, Labour Relations Act, 1995.
6 'Proposed Reform of the Ontario Labour Relations Act, A Discussion Paper from the Ministry of Labour' (Ontario: Ministry of Labour, Nov. 1991), 14.
7 The history of the legal treatment of domestic workers in Canada until 1940 is drawn from Cunningham (1991).
8 For a discussion of the statistics, see Cunningham (1991, 24–5).
9 Cunningham (1991, 54–8). As Cunningham recounts, there were also small numbers of domestic workers from places other than Europe. The first Caribbean domestic scheme implemented from 1910 to 1911 brought 100 women from Guadeloupe to Quebec. But despite the constant demand for domestic workers, race appears to have outweighed economic interest. Between 1904 and 1931 only 2,363 Caribbean blacks were admitted – largely as labourers and domestics (Cunningham 1991, 58). See also Calliste (1991, 95).

10 Minimum-wage legislation enacted in Alberta, Manitoba, Saskatchewan, Quebec, Nova Scotia, British Columbia, and Ontario excluded domestic workers (Cunningham 1991, 131–2).
11 Despite the Depression, the Workers Unity League, which was the trade union wing of the Communist Party of Canada, was active in organizing workers, including domestics (Cunningham 1991, 136–9). See generally, Palmer (1992, 253–5).
12 An Act to Provide for Collective Bargaining, S.O. 1943, c. 4, s. 24(b).
13 Senate Report no. 573, 2306.
14 The exclusion of domestic and agricultural workers from all of the New Deal labour protections was part of a political pact to ensure that Southern Democratic Senators supported Roosevelt's New Deal policies. For a discussion of the exclusion of domestic workers from the Social Security Act, 1935, see Gordon (1994, 5, 22, 133–4, 275–6). For a discussion of the exclusion of agricultural workers, most of whom were black, from The Fair Labor Act, 1938, see Anderson (1989, 649–67) and Linder (1987, 1335–93). Domestic workers were also excluded from this legislation, see Goldberg (1990, 63–104). Note, however, that Linder (1987, 1336, note 12) claims that the only possible exception to the explicit institutionalization of racially based exclusions in labour legislation may have been the exclusion of agricultural workers from the National Labour Relations Act, 1935.
15 Interview with Fely O. Villasin, Co-Ordinator, INTERCEDE, Toronto, 20 May 1994.
16 The Women's Legal and Education Action Fund (LEAF) organized and took a constitutional challenge to the regulation on behalf of INTERCEDE and two domestic workers (Chittenden, Villahouva, The Toronto Organization for Domestic Workers' Rights v. The A.G. of Ontario). Prior to the commencement of the proceedings, the current regulation was introduced. Although there was a partial redress of the overtime exemption, domestic workers continued to be exempted from the maximum hours of work protections.
  In British Columbia, a petition challenging the validity of a regulation issued under the Employment Standards Act (B.C. Reg37/81, s. 9(r)) that exempted domestic workers from overtime provisions was challenged on the ground that it violated s.7 of the Charter of Rights and Freedoms, which provides that 'Everyone has the right to life, liberty and security of the person and the right not to be deprived thereof except in accordance with the principles of natural justice.' In dismissing the petition, the Court asserted that s. 15 of the Charter, which provides equal treatment before and under the law as well as equal benefit under the law, was not in effect at the time

the petition was argued before the court; Domestic Workers' Union v. A.G. B.C.; (1984) 1 D.L.R. (4th) 560 (B.C.S.C.).

17 Employment Standards Act, R.S.O. 1990, c. E.14, s. 24. The only protection domestic workers have is that employers are obliged to provide them with two periods of free time each week; one of 36 consecutive hours and one of 12 consecutive hours, which may be, but need not be, consecutive with each other. If the domestic worker consents to work during a free period, that time is to be added, at a rate of 1.5 hours for every hour spent working during a free period, to one of the required free periods during the next four weeks or compensated at the rate of 1.5 times the regular hourly rate.

18 Suzanne Silk-Klein, director of policy for the Ontario Ministry of Labour, conceded that there are many compelling reasons why domestic workers would hesitate before filing an employment standards complaint; as quoted in Macklin (1993, 724).

19 Interview with Fely O. Villasin, Co-ordinator, INTERCEDE, Toronto, 20 May 1994.

20 For example, see the Open Letter to the Minister of Labour on the Approach of the Current Government to Labour Law Reform, dated 3 February 1992, which was signed by representatives of INTERCEDE, the Campaign for Fair Wages and Working Condition for Homeworkers, Chinese Canadian National Council Women's Issues Committee, Equal Pay Coalition, National Action Committee on the Status of Women, Older Women's Network, Ontario Coalition for Better Child Care, Ontario Women's Action Coalition.

21 See, for example, the National Action Committee on the Status of Women's and the Ontario Federation of Labour's written responses to the Ontario Ministry of Labour's Discussion Paper of Labour Law Reform.

22 The response by business groups is briefly sketched in White (1993, 200–3).

23 Project Economic Growth, a 160 member-strong coalition of companies founded to oppose the NDP's proposed labour law reforms, took out advertisements in major Ontario dailies, on the radio, and television and purchased billboard space to attack the reforms canvassed in the leaked cabinet document. See, for example, Lester (1991).

24 Highlights, Labour Relations Act Reform, An Outline of the Original Proposals, the Impact of Consultation, and the Government's Changes (Ontario: Ministry of Labour, undated) p. 2 of proposals for change.

25 Ontario Labour Relations Act, R.S.O. 1990, c.L.2, s. 6(1).

26 Under both the Foreign Domestic Movement program and its successor, the Live-in Caregiver Program, domestic workers are required to live in their

employer's residence as a condition of immigration. For a discussion of the requirements under the two programs see Jackman (1993).

27 The other provinces are Ontario, except for the period between 1993 and 1996, Alberta, and New Brunswick.

28 In British Columbia in the late 1970s a trade union for domestic workers, called the Domestic Workers' Union (DWU), was formed. The DWU worked on establishing a hiring hall for domestic workers and obtaining a first contract. This proved to be extremely difficult. See Epstein (1983, 235).

29 For a discussion of domestic employment agencies see Bakan and Stasiulis (1995, 303–35).

30 The Coalition included a number of advocacy groups, including a union, a legal clinic, organizations representing visible minority workers, and social justice and women's groups. For a discussion of the Coalition and its tactics, see Boroway, Gordon, and Lebans (1993, 299).

31 The coalition of Women for Labour Law Reform was very active in lobbying for broader-based bargaining and received some support from the labour movement. Using the examples of homeworkers in the garment industry and domestic workers, the Coalition and its member groups emphasized the need for broader-based bargaining structures to break down the isolation of women who worked for wages in the home. The aim was to call the government to account for its equity agenda to improve the working conditions of workers who were women, members of visible minorities or both, at the bottom of the labour market by focusing on homeworkers and domestic workers.

32 For detailed recommendations refer to the report, entitled *Meeting the Needs of Vulnerable Workers* (Ontario District Council 1993).

33 For a discussion of the legislation and the political reaction to it see Panitch and Swartz (1993) and Walkon (1993, 24).

34 Statement by the Honourable Elizabeth Witmer, Minister of Labour for Ontario, Re: Introduction of Bill 7 (An Act to restore balance and stability to labour relations and to promote economic prosperity), Queen's Park, 4 October 1995.

35 Labour Relations Act, 1995, S.O. 1995, c. 1; Ontario Ministry of Labour, Labour Relations Amendments, Fact Sheet: On the Workplace Democracy Amendments, October 1995.

36 Submission to the Minister of Labour on the Repeal of the Bill 40 reforms and other proposed changes to the Labour Relations Act, 22 August 1995.

37 For a discussion of the Live-in Caregiver Program which has governed the immigration status of foreign domestic workers since 1992 see Bakan and Stasiulis (1996, 228–9) and Macklin (1994, 26–9).

5

'The Work at Home Is Not Recognized': Organizing Domestic Workers in Montreal

MIRIAM ELVIR

Miriam Elvir is a member of L'Association pour la Défense des Droits du Personnel Domestique [The Association for the Defence of the Rights of Domestic Workers]. She has served as a board member and as an employee, responsible for the first two years of the placement service run by the association. This article is based on a series of interviews with Ms Elvir conducted by Daiva Stasiulis between 1994 and 1996. Also present at one 1994 interview, assisting with the translation (from French to English), and contributing to the discussion was Denise Caron, the current coordinator of the Association.

Ms Elvir had acquired her Canadian citizenship status over the course of the interviews. She reported:

> I feel happy to be able to use my real name, something that I felt I couldn't do when I was merely a landed immigrant. Even if we are landed, we do not have permanent status because we have had to experience the fear and vulnerability of temporary status. It takes time to regain confidence in ourselves. No one says that you can't say what you want to say, but the insecurity and fear are there.

Background: The Path to Migrant Labour

I was a Spanish teacher in a French-Spanish school for two and a half years in my country in Latin America. Since I was fourteen years old, I had been active in the student movement. As a teacher I was always active in the federation of teachers at the national level. The board of the school thought it was better to have a teacher who was not engaged in politics, so they found a way to push me out. After I lost that job, I went to sell books.

In May 1988, there was a big problem in my country. The U.S. embassy was fire-bombed. One month later, I talked to a friend who lived in Montreal. She asked me, 'Why don't you come to Montreal, where you can learn French and then come back to work as a French teacher?' I already spoke a little French. My friend sent me a letter of invitation. And in two months, I had my papers and travelled to Canada as a visitor. It was all very fast.

I was in Montreal for six months as a visitor, and was looking for the best way to get my immigration papers. My Canadian friends told me: 'If you get a contract in a home, you can get landed after two years.' For me, it was the best opportunity, because I always worked with kids. I am a teacher. And in my country, we feel that kids in Canada are very well treated. The people who work with kids are important people. And I thought that I could be a teacher in a private home.

I never thought that I would have to serve at a table. But I didn't know about the domestic worker program at that time. So I applied as an independent worker for one year. My friends found someone who needed a babysitter. The employer sent my papers to New York and I had to go there for an interview.

Crossing the Canadian Border

Quebec accepted me, because I sent my résumé, but Canada refused me. They said with my education – two years of university and a lot of diplomas from my home country – I could not do the job as a domestic worker.

After I came back to Quebec from my interview in New York, I challenged the federal government's decision with the aid of a lawyer. We asked for another interview to be conducted in French in New York, because I did not feel comfortable during the interview conducted in English. I was unable to properly explain my experience or my situation. After that, I was accepted by Quebec and the federal government.

I was given a work permit for one year with that employer. But I was still not in the federal program. After one year, the lady I worked for didn't need me any more. So I had to find another employer. I went to Honduras for a vacation, but I wanted to come back to Canada. I knew at that time that my status had changed and that if I wanted to renew my work permit, I had to get involved in the foreign domestic worker program.

I got my next job through a newspaper advertisement. My second employer in Canada was a woman who started to file for my papers. It was in Toronto. I didn't like Toronto. She started to pay me under the table before I got my papers. She was from a business family. I had to look after a three-year-old boy, whom I was supposed to teach French, English, and Spanish – like a teacher. I also had to travel to New York with this family for weekend business trips.

I had to put on a uniform. I felt like a servant. I never, never imagined that I would be treated like this. I was well paid, but first they told me that I would have the weekend off every two weeks. Then they would tell me, 'You're not going to go out this weekend. Could you go out Wednesday during the morning?' So they started to cut short my time off.

I used to say it was like the *Dallas* world, the television soap opera, because the richest people met at this house. My employers asked me to receive the guests. When visitors came during the fall and wore boots, after they rang the doorbell I was to open the door and they expected me to take off their boots. I had to do all this. And the first time I did, I went to my room and I cried. I said, 'No, no, no!' I went to see the woman who worked there before me, and she said, 'But the guests are going to give you an envelope with tips.' It wasn't worth the money. I told my employer, 'I can't do this.'

When I finished my work, I went to my room and I took off my uniform, even if I wasn't going out. My employers told me, 'If you want to stay at home, you'll have to be always in uniform.' I said no. I was always a rebel.

So I decided to stop the papers. At the time, they were almost completed, but I said to myself, 'No, I cannot accept this.' It was an awful experience; it was the worst.

I came back to Montreal, and I had to start all the papers again. I found another employer who was an immigration lawyer. He offered to give me a job to take care of his mother, who was very ill. The condition was, 'If you work for one year, you don't have to pay anything. But if you quit, you must pay me a fee of $1,500.' This was because the lawyer had to go outside the country to Atlanta to get my papers. I accepted, and he enrolled me in the federal program.

But my job disappeared when the lawyer's mother died. He asked me to drive his kids to school, but for that I had to get a driver's licence. I tried to get it, but I didn't. I thought that it was a lot of responsibility. So we finished the contract, and he said that I had to pay the fee.

I found this unjust as I was unable to do the job. So I went to see another lawyer to try to contest this. The lawyer told me that I didn't have a chance, given that my former employer was an immigration lawyer. So we made an arrangement, that I would have to pay $150 a month. Fortunately, after six months of payments at which time I got married, my former employer cancelled the balance of my debt. My employer proposed to make changes for a new contract for me, but I started to look for another job.

It was at this time that I became involved with the Association. They tried to find me a new employer. I also went to a placement agency, and the woman there tried to find a job for me. They found a lady who I would work for while she filed the papers. It was under the table. Until I had my permit, I was working illegally. This made me afraid every day. I knew that I was illegal and if there was someone I didn't like at home or at work, I couldn't say anything, because my employer could say, 'Okay, you go. It's finished. No contract.'

We don't have any power to negotiate under these circumstances. I worked for her for just three months. I had to do everything for her, from 8:00 in the morning until 11:00 at night. I lived Monday to Friday at my employer's, and Friday night to Sunday I stayed at my friend's home. The first week, I got a cheque for $90; the second week, I got a cheque for $60; and the third week, I got a cheque for $30.

When I tried to negotiate with the lady, she told me that the agency that placed me knew that it was a temporary job. Her mother was in Italy, and she had now come back. When I got my papers, the lady said to me, 'Oh, I'm sorry but I can't guarantee your job any more.'

I made photocopies of the cheques, brought them to the Immigration office and showed them to the agent there. He just laughed. He said, 'Oh, you have to change. If there is no job for you, you have to change.' It was terrible because I had to pay the lawyer, my former employer, $150 a month. I had to borrow money every time I lost a job. We also have to pay the federal government $100 every time we change a work permit, and now we also have to pay $100 to the government of Quebec. Two, three months without a cent is not easy.

Working as a Domestic in Canada

So I had to start again, to find another job, another employer who would make me an offer at the Employment Centre. This time, I found a family I really appreciated, my last employers while I worked as a domestic. I worked for them for fourteen months. They were two doctors. I took care of three children: three girls, eighteen months, three years, and six-and-a-half-years old. It was a very good job in relation to the others. They offered me $300 a week – I had never seen this before. I had to work hard. They expected a lot. And at this home, I was not only looking after the kids, but also the home. My day started at 8:00 AM and finished at 6:00 PM.

My schedule was always full. I worked fifty hours per week. I had to drop the kids off at school and pick them up. I had to go to the gym. By this time, I had my driver's licence. We arranged a car pool with the neighbours. Sometimes, I had five or six kids. Or when the neighbours had problems, they brought me their kids. There were always a lot of kids at home. I had to clean the house, to look after the children, prepare the meals, go to the supermarket – everything. Sometimes it was a little difficult with the kids. They started to say 'Mummy said yes to this. You say no.' When I came back on Monday after the weekend, the kids behaved differently. Because during the week, we can control the kids, but during the weekend they can do anything they want. So Monday was always a new start.

And the couple went away for a full week while I stayed at home with the kids. Sometimes I even worked on the weekends. Sometimes I had to work seven days a week. I was very, very active. But I got paid overtime. I loved the job and I did it with passion. It was physically very hard and I was tired when I finished. But the treatment was different. I knew that the family was thoughtful. It was a job, a real job where I felt I was a worker.

Of course I felt different when visitors came, when their family came to visit. With my employer, we could talk, and we could take a cup of tea. But when there were visitors, I had to just serve. It was embarrassing. When they had visitors, at meal times, my employers would say, 'Come, come have a seat.' But I didn't want to join them. There is always distance, as if they put up a wall. There were barriers at home. Domestics have their place. We will never be part of the family, even if we have been told that we are.

My room was in the basement. Every time, it was in the basement. But it was okay. And after I finished my job, I could leave and go to the library to study. I was studying accounting by mail.

Finally, when my husband, a refugee from Panama, received his landed immigrant status, it was mine too.

Advocating Domestic Workers' Rights

It was when I had problems with my employer, the immigration lawyer, that I became involved with the association. I didn't know that there was an association of domestic workers. When I went to see a lawyer, she told me that I couldn't do very much about the fee my employer was charging me, but that I could go to the association and see what I could do. So I came to the association. And effectively they told me that there wasn't much I could do because my employer was a lawyer and because it would take too much time and energy. The best thing for me would be to find another job and start again. But they invited me to come to the meetings.

When I started at the association, I saw the limitations we have. I met more domestic workers and I found that they had a lot of problems – more than I have had – and worse. There were people who were in crisis, who cried, who were depressed. People who were being sexually harassed, all kinds of problems. So I knew I wasn't alone. And at the same time, it was a place where I could express myself freely. We could go through a week at work, but after that came the weekend, and we could bring out our frustrations. This is why I found the meetings interesting and I continued in the association.

When there was a threat that the government would abolish the foreign domestic worker program, we had to make a brief. We organized all the members to contest the law. And after that I was on the board for one year. The board is two-thirds domestics and one-third other people who are involved. I also went to a weekend training session. The association conducts training sessions twice a year.

There are a lot of workers in other areas who have other kinds of problems. It's not just domestics. But the question is who is going to defend domestic workers?

The problem is that the work of people at home is not recognized, whether it is paid or unpaid. This is because this society devalues housework. Since I started working as a domestic, I never felt that I was a person, a real worker, until my last employer. At the association we are trying not to use the term 'domestic worker' because when I think of domestic worker, I think of domesticity and being domesticated. We prefer to say 'home caregiver.' I don't think that the fact of a change in name is going to change the situation. But it's going to help women realize that they are important people.

The employer makes lists of things to do. But often the employer doesn't know the job. They don't have any idea about the job. The worker knows the job better than the employer. Also, looking after children is a big responsibility. It's not just a question of playing with the kids for a couple of hours; the home is the first school for kids. I have always said, if the conditions were better, I would continue to do the job. I love kids. I can do the job in a home. It's a job. But with current conditions, the relations between the employer and the worker are unequal.

It's difficult to change these conditions. Change is not going to start today, and be finished tomorrow. But I think that household workers must be trained to gain confidence, and to do their job like any other job. Also the employers have to be educated to understand that they need to show respect. If they need somebody to work in their home, there should be a schedule as there would be for any other employee; when that work schedule is finished, overtime starts. Since the employers don't accept this under this program, it's difficult.

This is especially so because in Canada they hire people from other countries who come here to work for a salary. When they arrive, they don't know where to go; they don't know what to do. There is surveillance. They – Immigration, employers, society – watch the work done by the worker. But who is going to regulate the employer?

We come with a contract for one year, and the immigration status is precarious. Individually, people who leave their countries come to work to earn money. This is a way to help their families and improve their home lives, and this affects the mentality of these people. Someone who in her home country was aware of the reality of the conditions there is more easily going to become aware of the situation here. But if someone comes here just to work and earn money, sometimes she is going to close her eyes and say, 'No, this is not my problem. I don't want to mix it up.' I think that the association has started to move to contest some of these political issues.

Our employers are rich. They have money, power, everything. So we can't fight them. We think that the best way to improve conditions is to train household workers to help them to become aware about who they are and where they want to go. This is the only way to change the situation.

Placement Agencies, Union Rights, and Organizing Domestic Workers

The association has recently developed a project for the placement of household workers. We have seen the problems that household workers have when they go to the agencies to find an employer. The agency usually cares only for the money they collect from the employer, and they don't care about what is going to happen to the worker. In our association, we thought that if we work, we can find employers and do some follow-up.

We applied for a grant to support a project to form our own placement agency. It took one year to receive an answer. We were funded for one year by the Societé Québécoise Dévelopement de la Main d'Oeuvre. I was hired to work on this project. Volunteers are also involved: people working on the computer, who provide translation, and so on.

We have also been involved in establishing a contract between employers and employees. That is a big step because at least now home caregivers will have a contract. The household worker has the legal right to know the specific tasks expected; if she doesn't want to do one task, she can say no. If the employers have a swimming pool, for example, or if there is a pet in the house, the worker is free to say, 'I don't want to take that responsibility.' During the first year of the placement agency, there were seventeen contracts signed with employers. But what is more important, we have offered nine orientation sessions for the home caregivers with a total of sixty-six participants. We have received many calls from both employers and employees. So we had an opportunity to convey information on the laws covering home caregivers even among those who did not use our services. This year was also important for developing skills and knowledge within the association of the needs of home caregivers, and a better knowledge of the market. I think that we have built a good reputation as a placement agency. Our objective is to get the home caregivers more involved in the running of the agency. We are currently evaluating the results of the second year to decide whether we will continue as a placement service or develop a cooperative (where home caregivers would be involved in the management and feel responsible for the success of the enterprise).

Unpaid salaries, or lack of payment for overtime, are the main problems home caregivers encounter. We learned of several people who were earning a net salary and the employer was supposed to send money to the government. When the workers received the forms for income tax returns, there had been no deductions made or there had been a difference between the amount deducted and the amount sent to the government. Sometimes, the home caregiver had to pay that difference from her pocket. Ninety per cent of the workers we ask do not even receive a pay slip.

There are laws, but we can't use them. We go to the Immigration office and they say, 'Oh, it's not my responsibility, it's not under my jurisdiction.' We go to Labour Standards and they say, 'Oh, we can't do anything.' Another problem for household workers in Quebec is that they have to pass an interview in French in order to become landed, even for those people who come in with English. So they have to take French courses on the weekend. Even though they have a long work schedule, they have to come on the weekend – not because they want to study French, but because they have to pass an interview.

The association also tried to unionize, but it is very difficult. The Labour Standards department told us that the employers are independent – there are no corporations or companies. So if we want to unionize household workers, we have to regulate the employers. Who is going to do that? At this moment, the only thing we can do is to reinforce the organizations of the household workers, like this association. The association has to participate with other organizations across Canada, and even internationally. We have some links with organizations in the United States and Latin America – mostly receiving information and learning about their struggles.

In February 1995, we sent a brief to the Quebec minister of employment where we asked for seven changes to employment standards. These changes included adopting the term, 'home caregiver' instead of 'domestic'; eliminating the the difference in salary between live-in and live-out caregivers; providing 'live-in' caregivers with the same number of hours of work as 'live-out'; including babysitters in the law [currently not all people who take care of children, such as elder (over 65) and handicapped caregivers, are covered under the law]; including caregivers under Quebec health and safety legislation; registering employers of home caregivers under the Labour Standards legislation; and asking for penalties against employers who fail to respect the laws covering home caregivers. We met with the minister, Louise Harel, who urged us to get support for these changes. We have targeted a lot of groups and have received support from the Fédération des Femmes du Québec (FFQ), le Conseil de la Famille, and many other groups.

After we met with the minister, Mme Harel nominated me to the Labour Standards Board. Since March 1995, I have sat on the board as a representative of non-unionized workers and the cultural communities. My work as a member of the board has helped to create greater awareness within the government and public at large of the issues affecting home caregivers. It has also permitted me to become better acquainted with the reality of workers in general.

There are many things that can change. For example, the fact that they ask for twenty-four months of live-in work. And the fact that if a woman is pregnant, she is penalized. Mexican workers who come as agricultural workers don't have this problem. Why? Because they are men; they are never going to be pregnant.

And I detest, I hate it that on the work permit there is the name of the employer. When I first saw the name of my employer on my work permit, I felt like property. This is another thing that we can change.

6

'We Can Still Fight Back': Organizing Domestic Workers in Toronto

PURA M. VELASCO

Pura M. Velasco came to Canada as a domestic worker in 1989. From 1990 to 1992, she was president of INTERCEDE (the Toronto Organization for Domestic Workers' Rights). She is also a founding member of the Coalition for the Defense of Migrant Workers' Rights and Panday Sining, a musical collective of Filipino workers and students. After completing the required two years of live-in domestic service, Pura acquired landed immigrant status and is now employed as a community service worker in Toronto. The narrative below is based on a series of interviews with Pura conducted by Abigail B. Bakan between 1993 and 1996.

The Path to Migrant Labour

I was born in a barrio, but I went to Manila to go to the University of the Philippines, where I studied political science. I did not finish my studies because I became involved in organizing against the Marcos government with my partner, who was to become my husband. I worked in the left wing of the student movement and continued with my political involvement while raising my three children.

I left the Philippines for Saudi Arabia in 1981 to work as a medical transcriber in the largest industrial and military complex in Saudi Arabia . That's how I started as a migrant worker. I was an overseas contract worker there for four years, leaving my children with my husband. I would go back every year and visit my children. My youngest son was only five when I left.

After Saudi Arabia, I returned to the Philippines. But it was again the same situation – poverty and unemployment. There was nothing there for me to support my family, for them to have a decent life. I had no means to send my children to school, since at that time I was already a single mother. My marital relationship had changed over the years that I was working in Saudi Arabia.

After a few months of staying in the Philippines, I decided to go to Vienna, because I had a sister there. That was where I started working as a domestic worker, working for diplomats from the United Nations and United States embassy.

I entered Vienna as a tourist, and for a while I was on a student visa. While I was studying German at Vienna University, I was able to find jobs with some diplomatic personnel from the U.S. embassy. The American diplomats provided me with visas that were linked with their visas. So if they had visas for two years, mine would also last for two years.

My employment was on the condition that I would work for free as a domestic. I received no money. I had a room, but no board. I had to work part time for other members of the diplomatic community to support myself and my children in the Philippines doing various things like babysitting, housekeeping and waitressing for parties. After two years of doing various domestic work for the diplomatic circle in Vienna, I was offered a permanent domestic job by the U.S. Information Service Counselor's family and was paid by the U.S. State Department.

Crossing the Canadian Border

I came to Canada as a tourist, as I did when I went to Vienna. I wanted to leave Vienna right away because I did not feel secure without permanent residence status in the midst of a growing anti-immigrant sentiment among some of the local people there. I was looking for a permanent sanctuary for myself and my children. A lot of Filipinos were attracted to the United States, but I dreamt of having a life with my family in Canada. I heard a lot of positive things about Canada, that it was a more open, democratic, and welcoming country to immigrants. I was also impressed by its social policies and programs.

My plan was to stay in Vienna for only a few months and then go to Canada. I applied for a domestic position with a family from Hamilton, Ontario, who tried to sponsor me. Unfortunately, the Canadian immigration officer who interviewed me found me to be too smart to be a domestic worker. I could speak English better than the average applicant, according to her. I was naïve; I did not know that I was supposed to look stupid and unassertive. I thought that would be the end of it, and I did not expect to enter Canada after that.

I concentrated on working for the different American families that would come and go through Vienna. The last American family that I worked for helped me to get a U.S. visa. The moment I got my U.S. tourist visa, I went to the Canadian embassy in Vienna. I figured that the Canadians would trust me and grant me a visa once they saw my U.S. visa. And I was right.

As soon as I arrived in Toronto, I looked for a domestic job right away under the Foreign Domestic Movement (FDM) Program. I went to the same agency that had tried to get me a job with the Hamilton family when I was still in Vienna.

The first job that I got was with a very wealthy family, one related to the Reichman empire. This agency knew me from before, and they had seen my résumé. They gave me a choice of rich families, in wealthy neighbourhoods like Rosedale and Forest Hill, including the Campeau family and others. I chose the Reichman relations, because I'd read about the family in Vienna, when they were building the Canary Wharf project in London. I got on to the FDM program at that time.

Working as a Domestic in Canada

I worked for three other families after that first job. When I worked in Vienna, I did not feel as oppressed or as bonded to my employers as I did in Toronto. My experiences with the diplomatic people were different. Though my immigration status was vulnerable in Europe as it was in Canada, at work it was a liberal and more open relationship. They treated me more like a human being than when I was on the FDM. I had time off, a private room, and I was allowed to leave my workplace during my free time.

In Canada, I did not feel free. I had to live in my employers' homes, and could not leave my workplace even after work hours. My employers wanted to know where I was going at all times; they even checked the way I groomed myself. For some time, I accepted working long hours, delayed salary payments, and other forms of exploitation as part of the FDM requirements. I was very concerned about my immigration status.

I felt like a vacuum cleaner that my employers could use, silent and uncomplaining. They constantly reminded me that they sponsored me. Even the most liberal employer treated me like I was an object that she owned.

One night she told me how and where to watch the eclipse. When I told her that I would prefer to watch it on television so I could listen to the experts' explanation, she told me that she had every right to tell me how and where I should see the eclipse and that it was for my benefit. When I told my employer that I've watched eclipses all my life in the Philippines where the view of the sky and the moon was not obstructed by tall buildings and other unsightly aspects of the city, she got upset. She told me that I was not a Canadian, and therefore that I was an igno-ramus about eclipses.

All the employers who I worked for treated me as if I were their prop-erty to be shown off to people to enhance their status. One employer showed me off to her friends like I was a German- and English-speaking parrot. I only stayed at that job for a few days.

It is common for employers to be condescending and verbally abusive to their domestics. One of my employers once said, 'Oh, this is not typi-cal of a person in a domestic position to give her opinions even if she is not asked.' Employers expect the domestic to play dumb and be stu-pid, especially when the issues being discussed are wages or working conditions.

Advocating for Domestic Workers' Rights

As a domestic worker, I used to take children to the park where I learned from other nannies about my rights as a worker here in Canada. They also told me about INTERCEDE.

From my point of view, the two main problems with the Foreign Domestic Movement program – now called the Live-in Caregiver Pro-gram (LCP) – are the absence of landed immigrant status upon entering Canada, and the mandatory live-in condition for workers. These are the conditions that set up the workers in exploitative and vulnerable situations.

As a domestic under the FDM, I felt like a prisoner serving time for Immigration Canada and for my employers for almost three years. And what was my crime? I was poor and did not have the money to apply for landed-immigrant status. Several times I had experienced joining the long line-up of people waiting in the middle of the winter from 3:00 in the morning for the doors of the Immigration Canada office to open.

I dreaded going to the Immigration Office to work on my papers and approach sarcastic and intimidating Immigration officials. I had to undergo professional counselling to deal with my frustration when I was working as a domestic. My abhorrence for Immigration and Employment Canada was not unique. Filipino, Indian, and Caribbean domestic workers I knew were all haunted by the same monster, which very much controlled our stay in Canada.

If domestic workers were given the rights of landed immigrants when they entered Canada, just like other immigrant workers, it would lessen the inequality between the employer and the domestic workers. The workers would be more confident to assert their rights and negotiate for better working conditions. Also, if living in the employers' home was made optional, the workers would have a choice. They could leave an abusive employment situation without risking their status in the country. But these two conditions – temporary immigration status and compulsory living-in – make the employers believe that they own the workers.

The domestic workers program was set up to address only the needs of employers and Immigration Canada for cheap but efficient child care and elderly care; due consideration to the workers' welfare is not incorporated in the system. Based on many domestic workers' experiences with the FDM/LCP, the program violates the fundamental rights of the workers. This has to be challenged.

It is very important for domestic workers to be educated about their rights as workers and as human beings. Understanding the system and the society both locally and globally, and why we can never be part of our bosses' families, is very important. Stories shared among domestic workers about how they survive and struggle can help spark individual resistance.

But what is even more important is to get organized. We need to collectivize these cases of individual resistance. Immigration Canada will not easily give up the repressive temporary work-status scheme and the live-in requirement. And they will not easily alter the discriminatory criteria for participation in the LCP among workers from poor countries. Domestic workers should not be afraid to remind our bosses that we are human beings. We are not machines or animals. We feel pain, we get tired. And we also become angry.

On Union Rights, INTERCEDE, and Organizing Domestic Workers

In Ontario there was a token right for domestic workers to form a union under the previous NDP provincial government. This was granted in 1993, but it was reversed under the Conservative government three years later. Unfortunately, even when the labour law was amended to provide domestic workers with the right to collective bargaining, the Employment Standard Act (ESA) was not changed to facilitate unionization.

The former NDP government had provided some money for INTER-CEDE and the International Ladies Garment Workers Union (ILGWU) to do a study on collective bargaining. As long as the ESA is not amended, however, unionization even then was close to impossible. Based on research, the concept of a central registry was recommended as a mechanism that might possibly facilitate unionization (see Judy Fudge, this volume). But the onus was and is on the domestic workers to get organized. We have seen that legislation alone will not provide us with the means to strengthen ourselves collectively.

In addition to INTERCEDE, there are other organizations that have been doing organizing among domestic workers in Canada. In 1992, I had the privilege to meet with representatives from various different organizations across Canada when we had a joint lobby in Ottawa to fight against the discriminatory changes to the FDM. We established a network across the different provinces continued to meet informally. We have maintained links with organizations of Filipino domestic workers in Vancouver, Winnipeg, Montreal, and Ottawa, and in Alberta.

Politics from the anti-Marcos movement in the Philippines has a role to play among different domestic workers organizations within the Filipino community across Canada. So, for instance, if an organization is run by someone here in Canada who is seen as a conservative, on the right, in Filipino politics, someone who sees herself as on the left will tend not to touch them. They will not work together on domestic workers' rights issues here. This is a source of debate. I see it differently. I believe that to focus on these issues slows down the progress in mobilizing people.

In addition to Filipino domestics, INTERCEDE has caucuses of domestics from different places: Chinese and Indian domestics, for example. And I have very good relations with a number of Indian, Chinese, and Caribbean domestic workers. There is a very strong common identity that we are all being exploited.

We have continued the work of advocating not only for domestic workers, but for other migrant workers as well. Our Canadian network of Filipino domestic workers is now a member of an international Filipino migrant workers alliance, called Migrante. At the moment, Migrante and its allied organizations are in the midst of organizing Filipino migrants to counter the impact of globalization and to expose the Labor Export Policy of the Philippine government.

In Canada, while we address the immediate needs and issues that domestic workers are facing, we are also linking our campaign and work to the global struggle against the root causes of migration, poverty, and unemployment.

The Coalition for the Defence of Migrant Workers' Rights is another organization that has been established. It advances the rights of immigrant workers in Canada, including domestic workers. The coalition has participated in Migrante's protracted campaign for justice for Flor Contemplacion – the Filipino domestic who was unjustly charged with murder and hanged in Singapore in 1995 – and other migrant victims of injustices. The coalition is currently involved in a participatory research project to document our experiences. We are going to use this research to advocate changes in policies affecting domestics and other migrants both locally and internationally.

Canada and the International Situation

A lot of women are very grateful about getting a job as a domestic worker in Canada. The usual argument that I encounter in talking to domestic workers here about their rights in Canada is that they believe they 'owe' something to their employers because they were given this 'opportunity.'

This is why it is difficult to get across the fact that, really, Canada is not the compassionate country that it is portrayed to be internationally. Domestic workers are not here for humanitarian reasons. It's not from the bottom of their hearts that this government wants to help us. This is posturing. It is difficult sometimes for many domestic workers to recognize that we are here because they need us. There is a need to be met. The employers want cheap labour. If domestic workers have worked elsewhere, in the Middle East or Hong Kong, for example, this can be difficult for them to understand.

But look at the Live-in Caregiver Program (LCP). From a very personal stance, I was very happy that one of the criterion of the LCP, the requirement of a six-month formal training course as a condition for entry on the program, was altered to one year's experience equivalence. That change has been recognized. That's a personal victory, because I fought for that. Many of us fought for that to be changed. Domestic workers all across the country organized for that. Even if we don't get a lot of legislative changes at this point, even if we can't really change the LCP, many domestic workers today are becoming active.

I think education is the most important gain for domestic workers. And education and activism go together. We are learning that we have rights and demanding that they are respected. There are more and more of us who want to become activists around the issue of domestic workers and other human rights issues. That is the most satisfying victory that I feel, and I am very happy to see it. Now many more domestic workers know that they are being exploited. With these new people involved in organizing, more people will be active in the future.

Third World domestic workers come here and leave their own families. They pay taxes and yet they have to beg for social services here. They send money, and the International Monetary Fund (IMF) and the World Bank collect. Then poor countries have to beg for aid. It's our money you know. We've been supporting rich countries for so many years, out of the debts that we have been paying to the IMF and the World Bank. Back home, our families are supporting rich countries, through the debt service.

And now they understand this. I used to get scared sometimes and wonder, 'Why am I the only one thinking like this?' Now, I see a lot of new people who feel the same way. And it means that even if the government becomes more repressive, we can still fight back.

References

Abbate, Gay. 1995. 'Immigrants Challenge Ontario Law.' *Globe and Mail*, 18 April, A3

Abele, Francis, and Daiva Stasiulis. 1989. 'Canada as a "White Settler Colony": What about Natives and Immigrants?' In W. Clement and G. Williams, eds., *The New Canadian Political Economy*, 240–77. Montreal and Kingston: McGill-Queen's University Press

Abella, Manolo. 1992. 'International Migration and Development.' In G. Batistella and A. Paganoni, eds., *Philippine Labor Migration: Impact and Policy.* Quezon City: Scalabrini Migration Center

Aguilar, Delia D. 1988. *The Feminist Challenge (Initial Working Principles toward Reconceptualising the Feminist Movement in the Philippines).* Manila: Asian Social Institute

Aitken, Jennifer. 1987. 'A Stranger in the Family: The Legal Status of Domestic Workers in Ontario.' *Toronto Faculty of Law Review* 45/2 (Fall): 391–415

Alcid, Mary Lou, Ma. Lourdes, D.J. Maestro, Gina Alunan-Melgar, and Jorge Tigno. n.d. *The Impact of Overseas Employment on the Economic Status and Family Roles of Returned Filipina Domestic Workers from Hong Kong.* A Joint Study by the Friends of Filipino Migrant Workers, Inc. (KAIGIGAN) and the Mission for Filipino Migrant Workers – Hong Kong (MFMW)

Amin, Samir. 1990. *Maldevelopment.* London: Zed Books

Anderson, Patricia. 1991. 'Protection and Oppression: A Case Study of Domestic Service in Jamaica.' Institute of Social and Economic Research, University of the West Indies, Mona, Jamaica, August. Unpublished paper

Anderson, Patrick M. 1989. 'The Agricultural Employees Exemption from the Fair Labour Standards Act of 1938.' *Hamline Law Review* 12:649–67

Angeles, Leonora C. 1993. 'Between the Devil and the Deep Blue Sea: Transnational Issues and Trends in the Trafficking of Filipino Women.' A Philippine

Country Report, prepared for the 'Women Empowering Women: A Human Rights Conference on the Trafficking of Women in Asia,' Ateneo de Manila, April

Arat-Koc, Sedef. 1989. 'In the Privacy of Our Own Home: Foreign Domestic Workers as Solution to the Crisis in the Domestic Sphere in Canada.' *Studies in Political Economy* 28:33–58

– 1992. 'Immigration Policies, Migrant Domestic Workers and the Definition of Citizenship in Canada.' In V. Satzewich, ed., *Deconstructing a Nation: Immigration, Culturalism and Racism in the '90s Canada*, 229–42. Halifax: Fernwood Publishing

– 1993. 'The Politics of Family and Immigration in the Subordination of Domestic Workers in Canada.' In B. Fox, ed., *Family Patterns, Gender Relations*, 278–98. Toronto: Oxford University Press

Arat-Koc, Sedef, and Fely Villasin. 1990. *Report and Recommendations on the Foreign Domestic Movement Program*. Report prepared for INTERCEDE to be submitted to the Ministry of Employment and Immigration

Arat-Koc, Sedef, and Wenona Giles. 1994. 'Introduction.' In W. Giles and S. Arat-Koc, eds., *Maid in the Market: Women's Paid Domestic Labour*, 1–12. Halifax: Fernwood Publishing

Armstrong, Pat, and Hugh Armstrong. 1984. *The Double Ghetto: Canadian Women and Their Segregated Work*. Rev. ed. Toronto: McClelland & Stewart

Bakan, Abigail B. 1987. 'The International Market for Female Labour and Individual Deskilling: West Indian Women Workers in Toronto.' *North/South: Canadian Journal of Latin American and Caribbean Studies* 12/4:69–85

– 1994. 'Foreign Domestic Worker Policy in Canada and the Social Boundaries of Citizenship.' *Science and Society* 58/1:7–33 (reprinted in this volume)

– 1995. 'Making the Match: Domestic Placement Agencies and the Racialization of Women's Household Work.' *Signs: Journal of Women in Culture and Society* 20/2 (Winter): 303–35

Bakan, Abigail B., and Daiva Stasiulis. 1996. 'Structural Adjustment, Citizenship, and Foreign Domestic Labour: The Canadian Case.' In I. Bakker, ed., *Rethinking Restructuring: Gender and Change*, 217–42. Toronto: University of Toronto Press

Balibar, E. 1990. 'Paradoxes of Universality.' In D.T. Goldberg, ed., *Anatomy of Racism*, 283–94. Minneapolis: University of Minnesota Press

– 1991. 'Is There a Neo-Racism'? In E. Balibar and I. Wallerstein, eds. *Race, Nation, Class: Ambiguous Identities*, 17–28. London: Verso

Bals, Miriam. 1990. 'Being a Woman, a Domestic and a Temporary Worker in Quebec.' Master's thesis, Department of Social Work, University of Montreal

Barber, Marilyn. 1980. 'The Women Ontario Welcomed: Immigrant Domestics for Ontario Homes, 1870–1930.' *Ontario History* 72/3 (September): 148–72
- 1985. 'The Women Ontario Welcomed: Immigrant Domestics for Ontario Homes, 1870–1930.' In A. Prentice and S. Mann Trofimenkoff, eds., *The Neglected Majority: Essays in Canadian Women's History*, vol. 2, 102–21. Toronto: McClelland & Stewart
- 1986a. 'In Search of a Better Life: Scottish Domestics in Rural Ontario, 1900–1940.' *Polyphony* 8/1–2 (Special Issue on Women and Ethnicity): 13–16
- 1986b. 'Sunny Ontario for British Girls, 1900–30.' In Jean Burnet, ed., *Looking into My Sister's Eyes*. Toronto: Multiculturalism Historical Society of Ontario
- 1987. 'The Servant Problem in Manitoba, 1896–1930.' In Mary Kinnear, ed., *First Days, Fighting Days: Women in Manitoba History*, 100–19. Regina: Canadian Plains Research Center, University of Regina
- 1991. *Immigrant Domestic Servants in Canada*. Ottawa: Canadian Historical Association
Barrett, Michele, and Mary McIntosh. 1982. *The Anti-Social Family*. London: Verso/NLB
Bayefsky, Anne. 1980. 'The Jamaican Women Case and the Canadian Human Rights Act: Is Government Subject to the Principle of Equal Opportunity?' *U.W.O.L. Rev.* 18:461–7
BC Hansard. 1980. 22 August, 4173
Beckett, J. 1988. 'Aboriginality, Citizenship and the State.' *Social Analysis* 24
Board of Trade of Metropolitan Toronto. 1991. Submission on the Report of the Labour Relations Act Reform Committee, June
Bolaria, Singh and Peter Li. 1988. *Racial Oppression in Canada*. Toronto: Garamond Press
Bonacich, E. 1972. 'A Theory of Ethnic Antagonism: The Split Labour Market.' *American Sociological Review* 37:547–59
Borowy, Jan, Shelly Gordon, and Gayle Lebans. 1993. 'Are These Clothes Clean? The Campaign for Fair Wages and Working Conditions for Homeworkers.' In L. Carty, ed., *And Still We Rise: Feminist Political Mobilizing in Contemporary Canada*, 299–330. Toronto: Women's Press
Brand, Dionne. 1991. *No Burden to Carry: Narratives of Black Women in Ontario, 1920s-1950s*. Toronto: Women's Press
Brazeau, Ann. 1992. 'Introduction.' In S. Forbes Martin, ed., *Refugee Women*. ix–x. London: Zed Books
Bretl, Diana, and Christina Davidson. 1989. 'Background Paper: Foreign Domestic Workers in British Columbia.' Published by West Coast Domestic Workers Association
Briskin, Linda. 1980. 'Domestic Labour: A Methodological Discussion.' In

Bonnie Fox, ed., *Hidden in the Household: Women's Domestic Labour under Capitalism*, 135–72. Toronto: Canadian Women's Educational Press

Buckley, Suzanne. 1977. 'British Female Emigration and Imperial Development: Experiments in Canada, 1885–1931.' *Hecate* 3/2 (July): 26–40

Calliste, Agnes. 1989. 'Canada's Immigration Policy and Domestics from the Caribbean: The Second Domestic Scheme.' In Jesse Vorst et al., eds. *Race, Class, Gender: Bonds and Barriers*, 133–65. Toronto: Garamond Press and Society for Socialist Studies

– 1991. 'Canada's Immigration Policy and Domestic Blacks from the Caribbean: The Second Domestic Scheme.' In Elizabeth Comack and Stephen Brickey, eds., *The Social Basis of Law*, 95–121. 2nd ed. Toronto: Garamond Press

– 1993/4. 'Race, Gender and Canadian Immigration Policy: Blacks from the Caribbean, 1900–1937.' *Journal of Canadian Studies* 28/4:131–48

Canada. Citizenship and Immigration. 1993. *The Live-in Caregiver Program.* Ottawa: Ministry of Supply and Services

– 1996. *Employment Authorizations Issued Abroad under the Foreign Domestic Movement and Live-in Caregiver Program.* 30 April. Ottawa

Canada. Employment and Immigration. 1981. *Domestic Workers on Employment Authorizations: A Report on the Task Force on Immigration Practices and Procedures.* Ottawa: Ministry of Supply and Services

– 1992a. *The Live-in Caregiver Program: Information for Employers and Live-in Caregivers from Abroad.* Ottawa: Ministry of Supply and Services

– 1992b. For Release: Valcourt Announces New Live-in Caregiver Program. 27 April. Ottawa

Canada. Immigration and Colonization. 1929. *The Houseworker in Canada: Opportunities for Success, Work and Wages: Where to Go and What to Take.* Ottawa

Canada. Unemployment Insurance Commission. 1952. *Survey of Employment in Domestic Service in Canada.* Ottawa

Carty, Linda. 1994. 'African Canadian Women and the State: "Labour Only" Please.' In Peggy Bristow et al., eds., *'We're Rooted Here and They Can't Pull Us Up': Essays in African Canadian Women's History*, 193–229. Toronto: University of Toronto Press

Castro, Mary Garcia. 1989. 'What Is Bought and Sold in Domestic Service? The Case of Bogota: A Critical Review.' In E.M. Chaney and M. Garcia Castro, eds., *Muchachas No More: Household Workers in Latin America and the Caribbean*, 105–26. Philadelphia: Temple University Press

Chaney, Elsa J., and Mary Garcia Castro. 1989. 'Introduction: A New Field for Research and Action.' In E.M. Chaney and M. Garcia Castro, eds., *Muchachas No More: Household Workers in Latin America and the Caribbean*. 3–16. Philadelphia: Temple University Press

Childress, Alice. 1986. *Like One of the Family: Conversations from a Domestic's Life.* Boston: Beacon Press

Chunn, D. 1995.'Feminism, Law and Public Policy: Politicizing the Person.' In N. Mandell and A. Duffy, eds. *Canadian Families: Diversity, Conflict and Change.* 177–210. Toronto: Harcourt Brace

Cohen, Rina. 1987. 'The Work Conditions of Immigrant Women Live-in Domestics: Racism, Sexual Abuse and Invisibility.' *Resources for Feminist Research* 16/1:36–8

– 1994. 'A Brief History of Racism in Immigration Policies for Recruiting Domestics.' *Canadian Woman Studies* 14/2 (Spring): 83–6

Colen, Shellee. 1989. '"Just a Little Respect": West Indian Domestic Workers in New York City.' In E.M. Chaney and M. Garcia Castro, eds., *Muchachas No More: Household Workers in Latin America and the Caribbean*, 171–96. Philadelphia: Temple University Press

Conseil de Communautes culturelles et de l'immigration. 1992. 'Concerning the Draft Bill, "An Act to Amend the Act Respecting Labour Standards and Other Legislative Provisions."' Quebec: Submitted to the Committee on Social Affairs

Corelli, R. 1993. '"I'm Sorry about This": A New President Makes His First Mistake,' *Maclean's Magazine*, 106(5)

Cossman, Brenda. 1992. *'Family Inside/Out.'* Toronto: Feminist and Law Workshop Series

Cox, David. 1990. 'Children of Migrant Workers.' *Asian Migrant* 3/4 (October–December): 133–8

Cox, Robert. 1991. 'The Global Political Economy and Social Choice.' In D. Drache and M.S. Gertler, eds., *The New Era of Global Competition.* Montreal: McGill-Queen's University Press

Cunningham, Nicola. 1991. 'Seduced and Abandoned: The Legal Regulation of Domestic Workers in Canada from 1867 to 1940.' LLM thesis, York University

Daenzer, Patricia M. 1989. 'The Post-Migration Labour-Force Adaptation of Racial Minorities in Canada.' University of Toronto publication series: Working Papers on Social Welfare in Canada, no. 28

– 1991. 'Ideology and the Formation of Migration Policy: The Case of Immigrant Domestic Workers, 1940–1990.' Doctoral dissertation, Department of Social Work, University of Toronto

– 1993. *Regulating Class Privilege: Immigrant Servants in Canada, 1940s–1990.* Toronto: Canadian Scholars Press

Danys, Milda. 1986. *DP: Lithuanian Immigration to Canada.* Toronto: Multicultural Historical Society of Ontario

Deere, Carmen Diana (coordinator), et al. 1990. *In the Shadows of the Sun: Caribbean Development Alternatives and US Policy.* Boulder: Westview Press

DeVan, Mary Elizabeth. 1989. 'Social, Economic and Political Factors Influencing the Supply and Demand of Foreign Domestic Workers.' Master's thesis, Department of Anthropology and Sociology, University of British Columbia

'Domestic Worker Treated Like Slave.' 1992. *Globe and Mail,* 6 August, A6

Duarte, I. 1989. 'Household Workers in the Dominican Republic: A Question for the Feminist Movement.' In E.M. Chaney and M. Garcia Castro, eds., *Muchachas No More: Household Workers in Latin America and the Caribbean,* 197–219. Philadelphia: Temple University Press

Dudden, Faye. 1983. *Serving Women: Household Service in Nineteenth-Century America.* Middleton, CN: Wesleyan University Press

Elliot, Jean Leonard, and Augie Fleras. 1992. *Unequal Relations: An Introduction to Race and Ethnic Dynamics in Canada.* Scarborough: Prentice-Hall

Enloe, Cynthia. 1989. *Bananas, Beaches and Bases: Making Feminist Sense of International Politics.* Berkeley: University of California Press

Epstein, Rachel. 1983. 'Domestic Workers: The Experience in B.C.' In Linda Briskin and Lynda Yanz, eds., *Union Sisters,* 222–37. Toronto: Women's Press

Estable, Alma. 1986. *Immigrant Women in Canada: Current Issues.* Background paper, Canadian Advisory Council on the Status of Women, Ottawa

Eviota, Elizabeth U. 1990. 'The Articulation of Gender and Class in the Philippines.' In Eleanor Leacock and Helen I. Safa, eds., *Women's Work: Development and the Division of Labor by Gender,* 194–206. South Hadley, MA: Bergin and Garvey

'Ex-Pinoys Lose Right to Own Land in RP.' 1992. *Philippine Reporter.* 1–15 January, 1–2

Fairchilds, Cissie. 1984. *Domestic Enemies: Servants and Their Masters in Old Regime France.* Baltimore: Johns Hopkins University Press

Fairey, David. 1993. 'Vancouver Sectoral Bargaining Workshop.' *Just Wages* 3/2, 9–11

Fierlbeck, Katherine. 1991. 'Redefining Responsibility: The Politics of Citizenship in the United Kingdom.' *Canadian Journal of Political Science* 24/3:575–93

Flandrin, Jean-Louis. 1979. *Families in Former Times.* Cambridge: Cambridge University Press

Freeman, Jody. 1992. 'Defining Family in *Mossop v. DSS*: The Challenge of Anti-Essentialism and Interactive Discrimination for Human Rights Litigation.' *Feminism and Law Workshop Series.* Faculty of Law, University of Toronto, Toronto

Fruman, Leslie. 1987. 'Ontario's Domestics: The Fight for Basic Rights.' *Toronto Star*, 30 March, C1

Fudge, J.A. 1988. 'Voluntarism and Compulsion: The Canadian Federal Government's Intervention in Collective Bargaining from 1900 to 1946.' DPhil thesis, Oxford University

Gancayco, Emilio A., chair. 1995. *Presidential Fact-Finding and Policy Advisory Commission on the Protection of Overseas Filipinos; Report and Recommendation on the Delia Maga-Flor Contemplacion Case.* Submitted to President Ramos, 6 April. Manila, Philippines

Gavigan, Shelley A.M. 1992. 'Paradise Lost, Paradox Revisted: The Implications of Familial Ideology for Feminism, Lesbian and Gay Engagement to Law.' *Feminism and Law Workshop Series.* Faculty of Law, University of Toronto, Toronto

German, Lindsey. 1989. *Sex, Class and Socialism.* London: Bookmarks
– 1994. *Sex, Class and Socialism.* 2nd ed. London: Bookmarks

Gibson, Katherine, and Julie Graham. 1986. 'Situating Migrants in Theory: The Case of Filipino Migrant Contract Construction Workers.' *Capital and Class* 29: 130–47

Glenn, Evelyn Nakano. 1981. 'Occupational Ghettoization: Japanese American Women and Domestic Service, 1905–1970.' *Ethnicity* 7/4:352–86
– 1992. 'From Servitude to Service Work: Historical Continuities in the Racial Division of Paid Reproductive Work.' *Signs* 18/11:1–43

Goldberg, David Theo. 1993. *Racist Culture: Philosophy and the Politics of Meaning.* Cambridge, MA: Blackwell

Goldberg, Suzanne. 1990. 'In Pursuit of Workplace Rights.' *Yale Journal of Law and Feminism* 3: 63–104

Gordon, Linda. 1994. *Pitied but Not Entitled.* Toronto: Maxwell Macmillan Canada

Hall, Stuart, and David Held. 1989. 'Citizens and Citizenship.' In S. Hall and M. Jacques, eds., *New Times*, 173–90. London: Lawrence and Wishart

Harris, Ruth. 1988. 'The Transformation of Canadian Policies and Programs to Recruit Foreign Labour: The Case of Caribbean Female Domestic Workers, 1950s–1980s.' Doctoral dissertation, Department of Sociology, University of Michigan

Heap, Dan. 1992. 'Bill C-86: Why?' *Globe and Mail*, 13 August, A21

Heng, Geraldine, and Jandas Devan. 1992. 'State Fatherhood: The Politics of Nationalism, Sexuality and Race in Singapore.' In A. Parker et al., eds., *Nationalisms and Sexualities*, 343–63. New York: Routledge

Henry, Frances. 1968. 'The West Indian Domestic Scheme in Canada.' *Social and Economic Studies* 17/1: 83–91

Hook, Nancy. 1978. *Final Report. Domestic Service Occupation Study.* Ottawa: Ministry of Supply and Services

Horn, Pamela. 1975. *The Rise and Fall of the Victorian Servant.* Dublin: Gill and Macmillan

'Hundreds of RP Workers Exploited in Singapore.' *Manila Times,* 9 November, 3

Iacovetta, Franca. 1986. '"Primitive Villagers and Uneducated Girls': Canada Recruits Domestics from Italy, 1951–52.' *Canadian Woman Studies* 7/4: 14–18

– 1992. *Such Hardworking People: Italian Immigrants in Postwar Toronto.* Montreal: McGill-Queen's University Press

International Coalition to End Domestic Exploitation (INTERCEDE). 1983. 'Implementation of the Special Policy on Foreign Domestic Workers. Findings and Recommendations for Change.' A brief to the Minister of Employment and Immigration. Toronto

– 1989. 'Report and Recommendations for the Review of the Foreign Domestic Workers Movement Program.' Toronto

– 1992. 'Response to the Proposed Reform of the Ontario Labour Relations Act.' Toronto

Jackel, Susan. 1982. *A Flannel Shirt and Liberty: British Emigrant Gentlewomen in the Canadian West, 1880–1914.* Vancouver: University of British Columbia Press

Jackman, Barbara. 1993. 'Admission of Foreign Domestic Workers: An Overview of the Program.' Paper prepared for the 1993 Institute of Continuing Legal Education, *Feminist Analysis,* Toronto, 29 January

Jain, Harish C., and S. Muthuchidambaram. 1995. *Ontario Labour Law Reform: A History and Evaluation of Bill 40.* Kingston: McGill-Queen's University Press

Jong, Erica. 1993. 'A Culture That Loves Babies in Theory But Not in Practice.' *Globe and Mail,* 11 February, A25

Katzman, David. 1978a. 'Domestic Service: Women's Work.' In Ann Stromberg and Shirley Harkess, eds., *Women Working: Theories and Facts in Perspective,* 377–91. Palo Alto, CA: Mayfield Publishing Company

– 1978b *Seven Days a Week: Women and Domestic Service in Industrializing America.* New York: Oxford University Press

Knowles, Valerie. 1992. *Strangers at Our Gates: Canadian Immigration and Immigration Policy, 1540–1990.* Toronto: Dundurn Press

Kymlicka, Will. 1995. *Multicultural Citizenship: A Liberal Theory of Minority Rights.* Oxford: Oxford University Press

Lacelle, Claudette. 1987. *Urban Domestic Servants in Nineteenth-Century Canada.* Ottawa: National Historic Parks and Sites, Environment Canada – Parks

Law Union of Canada. 1981. *The Immigrant's Handbook*. Montreal: Black Rose Books

Layton-Henry, Zig, ed. 1990. *The Political Rights of Migrant Workers in Western Europe*. London: Sage Publications

Leah, Ronnie, and Gwen Morgan. 1979. 'Immigrant Women Fight Back: The Case of the Seven Jamaican Women.' *Resources for Feminist Research* 7/3:23–4

Lenskyj, Helen. 1981. 'A "Servant Problem" or a "Servant-Mistress Problem"? Domestic Service in Canada, 1890–1930.' *Atlantis* 7/1 (Fall): 3–11

Leslie, Genevieve. 1974. 'Domestic Service in Canada, 1880–1920.' In Janice Acton, ed., *Women at Work, 1850–1930*, 71–125. Toronto: Canadian Women's Educational Press

Lester, Lee. 1991. 'Coalition Fires Salvo at NDP,' *Toronto Sun*, 10 October

Light, Beth, and Ruth Roach Pierson. 1990. *No Easy Road: Women in Canada, 1920s to 1960s*. Toronto: New Hogtown Press

Linder, Marc. 1987. 'Farm Workers and the Fair Labor Standards Act: Racial Discrimination and the Law.' *Texas Law Review* 65:1335–87

Lindstrom-Best, Varpu. 1986a. 'Going to Work in America: Finnish Maids, 1911–1930.' *Polyphony* 8/1–2 (Special Issue on Women and Ethnicity): 17–20

– 1986b. '"I Won't Be a Slave" – Finnish Domestics in Canada, 1911–1930.' In Jean Burnett, ed., *Looking into My Sister's Eyes: An Exploration in Women's History*, 32–54. Toronto: Multiculturalism Historical Society of Ontario

Loney, Martin. 1993. 'Child-Care Problems.' [Letter to the Editor] *Globe and Mail*, 18 February, A24

Lycklama, Geertje. 1989. 'Trade in Maids: Asian Domestic Helpers in Migration Theory and Practice.' In Asian and Pacific Development Centre, ed., *Trade in Domestic Helpers: Causes, Mechanisms and Consequences*, 21–62. Kuala Lumpur: Asian and Pacific Development Centre

Mackenzie, Ian R. 1988. 'Early Movements of Domestics from the Caribbean and Canadian Immigration Policy: A Research Note.' *Alternate Routes* 8:124–43

Macklin, Audrey. 1992. 'Foreign Domestic Worker: Surrogate Housewife or Mail Order Servant.' *McGill Law Journal* 37/3:682–760

– 1994. 'On the Inside Looking In: Foreign Domestic Workers in Canada.' In Wenona Giles and Sedef Arat–Koc, eds., *Maid in the Market: Women's Paid Domestic Labour*, 13–39. Halifax: Fernwood Publishing

Marshall, T.H. 1950. *Citizenship and Social Class*. Cambridge: Cambridge University Press

Martin, P. 1995. 'Investment, Trade, and Migration.' *International Migration Review* 29/3:820–5

'Matchmaking Tips for Families and Nannies.' 1989. *National Nanny Newsletter*. 5/2:1–7

McBride, Theresa. 1976. *The Domestic Revolution: The Modernization of Household Service in England and France, 1820–1920.* New York: Holmes and Meir

McLaren, Angus. 1990. *Our Own Master Race: Eugenics in Canada, 1885–1945.* Toronto: McClelland & Stewart

Medel-Anonueva, C., L. Abad-Sarmiento, and Teresita Oliveros-Vistro. 1989. 'Filipina Domestic Helpers in Hong Kong and Singapore.' In Asian and Pacific Development Centre, ed., *Trade in Domestic Helpers: Causes, Mechanisms and Consequences.* Kuala Lumpur: Asian and Pacific Development Centre

Middle East Watch Women's Rights Project. 1992. 'Punishing the Victim: Rape and Mistreatment of Asian Maids in Kuwait.' Report 4/8 (August)

Migrante. 1996. Press Statement, Manila, 13 March

Miles, Robert. 1987. *Capitalism and Unfree Labour: Anomaly or Necessity?* London: Tavistock Publications

Mitchell, Alana. 1993. 'New Rules Create Greater Nanny Shortage.' *Globe and Mail*, 23 January, A5

Mittelstaedt, Martin. 1996. 'Ontario to Overhaul Labour Legislation.' *Globe and Mail*, 16 April, A1, A6

Mitter, Swasti. 1986. *Common Fate, Common Bond: Women in the Global Economy.* London: Pluto Press

Mitterauer, Michael, and Reinhard Sieder. 1982. *The European Family.* Oxford: B. Blackwell

Muszynski, Alicja. 1991. 'What is Patriarchy?' In Jessie Vorst et al., eds., *Race, Class, Gender: Bonds and Barriers*, 64–87. 2nd ed. Toronto: Garamond Press, 64–87

Ng, Roxanna. 1986. 'The Social Construction of Immigrant Women in Canada.' In Roberta Hamilton and Michele Barrett, eds., *The Politics of Diversity*, 269–86. Quebec: Book Centre Inc.

Ollenburger, Jane C., and Helen A. Moore. 1992. *A Sociology of Women: The Intersection of Patriarchy, Capitalism and Colonization.* Englewood Cliffs, NJ: Prentice-Hall

Ontario. 1991. 'Cabinet Submission Analysis and Policy Options, Reform of the Labour Relations Act: Policy Options and Analysis (confidential document prepared for the Ontario Cabinet).' 7 August

Ontario District Council of the International Ladies' Garment Workers' Union and INTERCEDE. 1993. *Meeting the Needs of Vulnerable Workers: Proposals for Improved Employment Legislation and Access to Collective Bargaining for Domestic Workers and Industrial Homeworkers.* Toronto

Ontario. Ministry of Labour. 1985. 'Study of Wages and Employment Conditions of Domestics and Their Employers.' Study conducted by Currie, Coopers & Lybrand, management consultants. Toronto

– 1991. *Partnership and Participation in the 1990's: Labour Law Reform in Ontario.* Report of the Labour Representatives to the Labour Law Reform Committee of the Ministry of Labour, 14 April

'Ottawa Revises Foreign Nanny Rules.' 1993. *Toronto Star*, 11 June, A10

Oziewicz, Estanislao. 1992a. 'Immigration Overhaul Sought.' *Globe and Mail*, 17 June, A1, A10

– 1992b. 'Proposals on Refugees Come Under Fire.' *Globe and Mail*, 18 June, A10

– 1992c. 'Immigration Proposal "not Canadian."' *Globe and Mail*, 19 June, A22

Palmer, Bryan D. 1992. *Working Class Experience.* 2nd ed. Toronto: McClelland & Stewart

Panitch, Leo, and Donald Swartz. 1993. *From Consent to Coercion.* 3rd ed. Toronto: Garamond Press

Parr, Joy. 1980. *Labouring Children: British Immigrant Apprentices to Canada, 1869–1924.* Montreal: McGill-Queen's University Press

Pateman, Carole. 1990. 'Promise and Paradox: Women and Democratic Citizenship.' Lecture at York University, 23 October, Toronto

Phillips, Paul, and Erin Phillips. 1983. *Women and Work: Inequality in the Labour Market.* Toronto: James Lorimer

Phizacklea, Anna, ed. 1983. *One Way Ticket: Migration and Female Labour.* London: Routledge & Kegan Paul

Pierson, Ruth Roach. 1986. *'They're Still Women After All': The Second World War and Canadian Womanhood.* Toronto: McClelland & Stewart

Portes, Alejandro, and John Walton. 1981. *Labor, Class and the International System.* New York: Academic Press

Prentice, Alison, et al. 1988. *Canadian Women: A History.* Toronto: Harcourt Brace Jovanovich

van Raaphorst, Donna L. 1988. *Union Maids Not Wanted: Organizing Domestic Workers, 1870–1940.* New York: Praeger

Radcliffe, S.A. 1990. 'Ethnicity, Patriarchy and Incorporation into the Nation: Female Migrants as Domestics in Peru.' *Society and Space* 8: 379–93

Richmond, Anthony. 1994. *Global Apartheid: Refugees, Racism, and the New World Order.* Toronto: Oxford University Press

Roberts, Barbara. 1976. 'Daughters of the Empire and Mothers of the Race: Caroline Chisholm and Female Emigration in the British Empire.' *Atlantis* 1/2: 106–27

– 1979. 'A Work of Empire: Canadian Reformers and British Female Immigration.' In Linda Kealey, ed., *A Not Unreasonable Claim: Women and Reform in Canada, 1880s–1920s*, 185–201. Toronto: Women's Press

– 1988. *Whence They Came.* Ottawa: University of Ottawa Press

– 1990. 'Ladies, Women and the State: Managing Female Immigration, 1880–

1920.' In Roxana Ng, Gillian Walker, and Jacob Muller, eds., *Community Organization and the Canadian State*. Toronto: Garamond Press, 108–38

Rollins, Judith. 1985. *Between Women: Domestics and Their Employers*. Philadelphia: Temple University Press

Romero, Mary. 1992. *Maid in the U.S.A.* New York: Routledge

Safire, William. 1995. 'The Hanging of Flor Contemplacion.' *Globe and Mail*, 25 April, A19

Salt, John. 1993. 'The Future of International Labor Migration.' *International Migration Review* 26/4:1077–111

Sassen-Koob, Saskia. 1981. 'Towards a Conceptualization of Immigrant Labor.' *Social Problems* 29/1:65–85

– 1984. 'Notes on the Incorporation of Third World Women into Wage-labor Through Immigration and Off-Shore Production.' *International Migration Review* 18/4:1144–67

Satzewich, Vic. 1989. 'Racism and Canadian Immigration Policy: The Government's View of Caribbean Migration, 1926–66.' *Canadian Ethnic Studies* 21/1: 77–97

– 1991. *Racism and the Incorporation of Foreign Labour: Farm Labour Migration to Canada since 1945*. London: Routledge

Scane, Joyce, and Marjatta Holt. 1988. *Immigrant Women: Their Untold History*. Toronto: OISE Press

Serwonka, Karen. 1991. *The Bare Essentials: A Needs Assessment of Foreign Domestic Workers in Ontario*. Toronto: INTERCEDE

Sherwell, Philip. 1995. 'Plight of Maid Wakens Philippine Anger.' *Globe and Mail*, 1 April, A1, A9

Shingadia, Ashwin. 1975. *Non-Immigrant Foreign Workers in Canada: A Preliminary Look*. Report prepared for Canada Department of Manpower and Immigration, October, Ottawa

Silvera, Makeda. 1983, 1989. *Silenced*. Toronto: Williams-Wallis Publishers (1984); Toronto: Sister Vision Press (1989)

Smith, Dorothy E. 1985. 'Women, Class and Family.' In Varda Burstyn and Dorothy E. Smith, eds., *Women, Class, Family and the State*, 1–44. Toronto: Garamond Press

Soysal, Yasemin Nuhoglu. 1994. *Limits of Citizenship: Migrants and Postnational Membership in Europe*. Chicago: University of Chicago Press

Stasiulis, Daiva. 1990. 'Theorizing Connections: Gender, Race, Ethnicity and Class.' In Peter S. Li, ed., *Race and Ethnic Relations in Canada*, 269–305. Toronto: Oxford University Press

Stasiulis, Daiva, and Glen Williams. 1992. 'Mapping Racial/Ethnic Hierarchy in the Canadian Social Formation, 1860–1914: An Examination of Selected

Federal Policy Debates.' Paper presented to the Annual General Meeting of the Canadian Political Science Association, Charlottetown, June

Stasiulis, Daiva, and Radha Jhappan. 1995. 'The Fractious Politics of a Settler Society: Canada.' In Daiva Stasiulis and Nira Yuval-Davis, eds., *Unsettling Settler Societies: Articulations of Gender, Race, Ethnicity and Class*, 95–131. Thousand Oaks, CA: Sage Publications

Strong-Boag, Veronica. 1985. 'Discovering the Home: The Last 150 Years of Domestic Work in Canada.' In Paula Bourne, ed., *Women's Paid and Unpaid Work: Historical and Contemporary Perspectives*, 35–60. Toronto: New Hogtown Press

Tesher, Ellie. 1995. 'Canada Must Protect Domestics.' *Toronto Star*, 31 March, A2

Timoll, Andrea L. 1989. 'Foreign Domestic Servants in Canada.' Honours Bachelor's thesis, Department of Political Studies, Queen's University

Torres-Calud, Edith G. n.d. 'Migration: The Philippine Experience (Rural to Urban; Country to Country).' *Awake 2* (Women, Migration and Sex Tourism)

Toughill, Kelly. 1996. 'Day-Care Funding Gets Mixed Review from Advocates.' *Toronto Star*, 11 May, A12

Townson, Monica. 1987. *Domestic Workers and the ESA*. Research report prepared for the Ontario Task Force on Hours of Work and Overtime, Toronto

Trager, Lillian. 1984. 'Family Strategies and the Migration of Women: Migrants to Dagupan City, Philippines.' *International Migration Review* 18/4:1264–77

Turner, Bryan S. 1990. 'Outline of a Theory of Citizenship.' *Sociology* 24:189–217

Turrittin, Jane S. 1976. 'Networks and Mobility: The Case of West Indian Domestics from Montserrat.' *Canadian Review of Sociology and Anthropology* 13/3:305–20

Ursel, J. 1992. *Private Lives, Public Policy: 100 Years of State Intervention in the Family*. Toronto: Women's Press

Valcourt, Bernard. 1992. Letter to Glenda P. Simms, PhD, president, Canadian Advisory Council on the Status of Women (CACSW) (courtesy of the CACSW), August 26

Valverde, Mariana. 1991. *The Age of Light, Soap and Water: Moral Reform in Canada, 1885–1925*. Toronto: McClelland & Stewart

van Kirk, Sylvia. 1977. 'The Impact of White Women on Fur Trade Society.' In Susan Mann Trofimenkoff and Alison Prentice, eds., *The Neglected Majority: Essays in Canadian Women's History*. Vol. 1, 27–48. Toronto: McClelland & Stewart

– 1983. *Many Tender Ties: Women in Fur-Trade Society, 1670–1870*. Winnipeg: Watson and Dyer

Villasin, Felicita, and M. Ann Phillips. 1994. 'Falling through the Cracks: Domestic Workers and Progressive Movements.' *Canadian Woman Studies* 14/2 (Spring): 87–90

Villasin, Fely. 1990. 'Domestic Workers from the Philippines: One-Month Observation Report.' Toronto: INTERCEDE

Walkon, Thomas. 1993. 'Some Contract. Some NDP Government.' Reprinted from the *Toronto Star*, 15 June, in *Canadian Dimension* (August), 24

West Coast Domestic Workers Association. 1989a. *West Coast Domestic Workers Association Newsletter* 2/10 (October)

West Coast Domestic Workers Association. 1989b. 'Brief to the Review Committee on the Foreign Domestic Worker Program: Foreign Domestic Workers in British Columbia – Recommendations for Change.' November

West Coast Domestic Workers Association. 1993. 'Brief to Employment Standards Act Review Committee.' March

White, Julie. 1993. *Sisters and Solidarity.* Toronto: Thompson Educational Press

Willes, J.A. 1979. *The Ontario Labour Court, 1943–44.* Kingston: Industrial Relations Centre

Young, Iris Marion. 1990. *Justice and the Politics of Difference.* Princeton: Princeton University Press

York, Geoffrey. 1992. 'Tory Politicians Form Family Compact.' *Toronto Star*, 8 June, A1, A4

Yuval-Davis, Nira. 1991. 'The Citizenship Debate: Women, Ethnic Processes and the State.' *Feminist Review* 39:58–68

Index